W9-AAP-770

Chasing GOD *Serving* MAN

Divine Encounters
Between Martha's Kitchen
and Mary's Worship

TOMMY TENNEY

Fresh Bread

An Imprint of

Destiny Image® Publishers, Inc.
P.O. Box 310
Shippensburg, PA 17257-0310

ISBN 0-7684-5007-1

For Worldwide Distribution
Printed in the U.S.A.

This book and all other Destiny Image, Revival Press, MercyPlace, Fresh Bread, Destiny Image Fiction, and Treasure House books are available at Christian bookstores and distributors worldwide.

For a U.S. bookstore nearest you, call **1-800-722-6774**.
For more information on foreign distributors, call **717-532-3040**.
Or reach us on the Internet: **www.destinyimage.com**

Dedication

To ushers and intercessors, to secretaries and singers.

To Bart and Coralee Pierce and to Tommy Barnett, who taught me much about serving man (even if from a distance).

To Ed Miller, Billy Cole, and Tom Barnes, who taught me much about serving God.

If sometimes I feel spiritually schizophrenic, torn between Mary's worship and Martha's service, these people help provide balance in my life.

To Billy Joe and Sharon Daughtery, for being midwives at the birthing.

To Thomas Trask, who demonstrates dignity while serving. To Elmer Towns, who whetted my appetite for writing—I honor you for the things I learned by our paths crossing.

To David and Nita, Brenda and Lloyd, Stephen and Sherrie, Karyn and Tiffany, for helping me keep balance in my private life.

To Mom and Dad, Jeannie and my three daughters, for teaching me balance is sanity.

Table of Contents

Prologue

Undoubtedly this will be the most controversial book I've ever written. Pursuers of revival will say, "Tommy has abandoned the pursuit." Socially conscious practitioners of compassion ministry will say, "Tommy has finally come to his senses." The truth is somewhere between Martha's kitchen and Mary's altar.

Martha and Mary are seemingly at eternal enmity. In this book, may there be a peace treaty. I have not abandoned the pursuit. I am at peace living in the middle—worshiping and working; chasing God, serving man.

Cast of Characters

Mary of the Alabaster Box—the sister who served Jesus with a bent knee, a broken heart, the worship of tears and precious anointing oil.

Martha of the Kitchen—the elder sister and owner of the family house, who, from the kitchen, faithfully served food, drink, and countless human comforts to Jesus and His guests.

Lazarus of the Empty Tomb—the brother of Mary and Martha, and the only man raised from the dead by a family Friend. (He was also the only man Jesus called His friend.)

Simon the ex-Leper and Holder of Banquets—the owner of the home where Mary and Martha provided Bethany's final feast for Divinity and humanity under one roof.

Judas Iscariot the disciple and betrayer of Jesus—the keeper of the money and the New Testament's most outspoken human critic of costly worship.

As Jesus and the disciples continued on their way to Jerusalem, they came to a village where a woman named Martha welcomed them into her home. Her sister, Mary, sat at the Lord's feet, listening to what He taught. But Martha was worrying over the big dinner she was preparing. She came to Jesus and said, "Lord, doesn't it seem unfair to You that my sister just sits here while I do all the work? Tell her to come and help me."

But the Lord said to her, "My dear Martha, you are so upset over all these details! There is really only one thing worth being concerned about. Mary has discovered it—and I won't take it away from her" (Luke 10:38-42 NLT).

Now Jesus loved Martha and her sister and Lazarus (John 11:5).

Six days before the Passover ceremonies began, Jesus arrived in Bethany, the home of Lazarus—the man He had raised from the dead. A dinner was prepared in Jesus' honor [at the home of Simon, a man who had leprosy]. Martha served, and Lazarus sat at the table with Him. Then Mary took a twelve-ounce jar of expensive perfume made from essence of nard, and she anointed Jesus' feet with it and wiped His feet with her hair. And the house was filled with fragrance.

But Judas Iscariot, one of His disciples—the one who would betray Him—said, "That perfume was worth a small fortune. It should have been sold and the money given to the poor." Not that he cared for the poor—he was a thief who was in charge of the disciples' funds, and he often took some for his own use.

Jesus replied, "Leave her alone. She did it in preparation for My burial. You will always have the poor among you, but I will not be here with you much longer [She has poured this perfume on Me to prepare My body for burial. I assure you, wherever the Good News is preached throughout the world, this woman's deed will be talked about in her memory]" (John 12:1-8 NLT, with details from Matthew 26:6-13 NLT).

Chapter One

Foxholes and Birds' Nests

From a Borrowed Womb to a Borrowed Tomb

Have you ever traveled to a distant destination only to discover that you forgot to make a hotel reservation? Every experienced traveler knows how it feels to arrive at a location only to learn the hotel has misplaced his advance reservation, leaving him with no accommodations for the night.

Jesus' first encounter as a human on earth began with a "No Vacancy" sign in Bethlehem, marking the beginning of His frustrating search for a welcome mat on earth. The truth is that He went from a borrowed womb to a borrowed tomb in search of a place to rest His head. The outrageous paradox of this picture is the fact that this was the Incognito Owner, the Divine Creator who was begging for enough hospitality to be born in the lowly realm of the created.

The manager of Hotel Bethlehem didn't know just who he had refused to host when he declined to make room for Joseph, Mary, and the holy babe. Perhaps he was following preset procedures or had little patience for disruptions of normal protocol. Is it possible he believed no advance reservation had been noted? (Never mind that the prophets had called ahead with the message, "The Messiah is coming," and specifically said He would arrive in Bethlehem, the city of David, the "house of bread."[1]) In any case, we know he told the expectant couple with the donkey, "Move on."

"The foxes have holes and the birds of the air have nests, but the Son of Man has nowhere to lay His head."

Isn't it odd that Jesus is *still* finding "No Vacancy" signs over so many "houses of bread" (churches) bearing His name today? They may be full of man but they are empty of God. They are filled to capacity with their established religious service procedures, meeting agendas, and pre-approved worship protocols.

These prestigious houses of worship proudly display their careful controls over what they view to be overwrought worshipers, religious extremism, and the dangers of unbridled passion. Whenever something or someone shows up at the door showing the signs of apparent spiritual pregnancy, they refuse to move man to make room for God. (There is nothing like passion showing up to make complacency feel threatened and out of place.) They promptly put up their "No Vacancy" signs and continue with church as usual while the visitation "moves on" in search of another place of habitation. A spiritual stable is preferred over the false fullness of man's motel.

The vagrancy of Divinity in the earth is painfully common to the Scriptures. Early in His ministry, Jesus warned a would-be disciple, *"The foxes have holes and the birds of the air have nests, but the Son of Man has nowhere to lay His head."*[2] I'm sad to say this passage still defines a chief obstacle blocking divine visitation.

DIVINITY INVADED HUMANITY FROM A LOWLY MANGER

Unknowingly, the lowly stable manager hosted Divinity that night in his small-town animal motel. The rest is "His-story"—a history transformed when Divinity invaded humanity from a lowly Bethlehem manger.

You never know who or what you are accommodating when you host humanity—it could be angels that catch you unaware.[3] Divinity may appear when you least expect Him. It pays to practice holy hospitality at all times. I believe the Gospel accounts of Jesus' arrival in Bethlehem would read differently today had that innkeeper in Bethlehem known whom he was turning away! I wonder how often our history would be transformed if we knew whom *we* turned away?

It seems glaringly obvious that mankind's mistake in failing to host the infancy of Jesus reappears as a reluctance to show hospitality for the maturity of the Messiah. The Bible accounts—and often the past and present practices in the Church—confirm this observation. We refused to believe at His conception, ignored Him at birth, and crucified Him at maturity. Such is the history of revival.

It appears that Mary and Joseph provided enough love and nurture to make the childhood of Jesus a comfortable one, but moments of awkwardness still arose due to His deity and divine mission.

We know that Jesus had an intense and extended encounter with the teachers of the Law in the temple at Jerusalem during the Feast of Passover in His twelfth year. We also understand that His single-minded devotion to "His Father's business" created an obvious tension that challenged the mostly earth-bound perceptions of Mary and Joseph:

> So when they saw Him, they were amazed; and His mother said to Him, "Son, why have You done this to us? Look, Your father and I have sought You anxiously." And He said to them, "Why did you seek Me? Did you not know that I must be about My Father's business?" But they did not understand the statement which He spoke to them.[4]

Already the awkwardness of the anointing began to feel more at home in the temple atmosphere of worship, yet He went home with humanity: "Then He went down with them and came to Nazareth, and was subject to them."[5]

THERE HAS NEVER BEEN A HEAD LIKE HIS HEAD!

Once Jesus left the home of His adolescence and launched His ministry in maturity, it became harder and harder to find a place of comfort. Why is this? Why was it easier for a fox to find a hole and for a bird to make a nest than for Jesus to find a place to lay His weary head? *Because there has never been a head like His head!*

Since the ministry requires me to spend so much time on the road, I often take along my wife and our daughters. On those occasions, my staff goes to great lengths to ensure that we reserve "connecting" hotel rooms. This allows my daughters to have their own room, while my wife and I have ours. We need to "play house" even while on the road.

After much very frustrating education, we learned that there is a distinct difference between "adjoining rooms" and "connecting rooms." Heaven help you if you or your hotel clerk doesn't understand that! We learned the hard way that even seasoned hotel personnel often do not understand the difference between "connecting" and "adjoining" rooms! (The definition seems simple enough: Adjoining rooms are next to one another but have no door between them, while connecting rooms share a common door that allows free movement between the rooms.)

While ministering in the New York City area, we found ourselves at the front desk of one of America's most respected hotel chains conducting a dialogue that was all too familiar:

"Pardon me, Ma'am, but the reservations clerk has made a mistake. We specifically requested *connecting rooms*, but that is not what you gave us."

"Well, we have you next to one another. Isn't that what you asked for?"

I felt the heat of frustration begin to rise, but I clenched my teeth and said, "Ma'am, you don't understand. I have young daughters with me tonight. I will not allow them to stay in a hotel room without my wife or I being there with them. That is unacceptable."

"Sir, we gave you *adjoining rooms*. That is all we can do."

"So what you're saying is, I'm going to be in one room alone tonight, so that my wife and my children can be together on the other side of a dividing wall?"

The clerk stammered a little before blurting out, "But they're right next to one another!"

"No," I said, "I want them to *connect*." Unfortunately, by that time of the evening, the night clerk couldn't do anything about it (although I am *sure* that she wanted to).

I reluctantly entered my *adjoining-but-not-connecting* room and wearily leaned against the inside doorway. Then I fixed my eyes on the blank wall space where the "connecting door" would have (and *should have*) been. The longer I stared at that wall, the more I missed my wife and daughters on the "other side." *Why am I doing this?* I thought. *The reason I brought my family along is so that I can be WITH them!*

Then my mind started working. "Wal-Mart is right down the street," I said aloud to myself. "Now I could get a power saw and fix this problem real quick! For a few dollars spent purchasing a saw, I could just cut a hole through that dividing wall and put in a connecting door right there...." Calculating the charges the hotel would add to my bill brought me back to reality. The money spent purchasing a saw was miniscule in comparison.

DIVINITY DEMOLISHED THE WALL THAT DIVIDES

Despite my brooding disappointment at the time, I didn't cut open a doorway that night. But the heavenly Father used that situation to remind me that He often feels the same way! I was reminded that He was so offended by a dividing wall that He really did create His own door. Through the obedience of His Son! I could almost picture Him saying, "Why should I put up with this? The reason I created humanity is so that I could be WITH them!"

God always has hated "veils." The first time He had the legal right He ripped the veil, rendering it irreparable and propping it

"Some may rightly point out that God Himself erected that protective wall, but God thought enough of the human race that He chose to "remodel" Heaven by creating a new and living "door of access" for all men through His Son."

open Himself. Paul told the Ephesians, "For He Himself...has broken down the middle wall of separation."[6] One translation says, "He tore down the wall."[7]

If God tore down a wall of separation, then that means there had to be a dividing wall that separated Him from His children in the first place.[8]

Some may rightly point out that God Himself erected that protective wall, but God thought enough of the human race that He chose to "remodel" Heaven by creating a new and living "door of access" for all men through His Son. Jesus told His disciples:

> *"Most assuredly, I say to you, I am the **door** of the sheep....If anyone enters by Me, he will be saved, and will go in and out and find pasture.*[9]

Do you know how much it cost God to "remodel" Heaven, to create that doorway? Sometimes, while sensing God's presence in worship, we proudly point out to Him what it cost us to be there. Remember that career, time, money, and pleasure are just tokens. Consider what it cost Him to visit with us in worship. Perhaps a revisiting of John 3:16 would put the cost of divine visitation in perspective:

For God so loved the world, that he gave his only begotten Son, that whosoever believeth in him should not perish, but have everlasting life.[10]

When the time came for God to tear down the middle wall between us, He didn't go to a hardware store or discount store and buy a "power saw." He tore down the wall legally by dividing or tearing the fleshly "veil" of His Son to create the divine doorway of access between Heaven and earth.

HOW MUCH DOES GOD HATE THINGS THAT SEPARATE?

Considering the great cost of our salvation, how much do you think God hates things that separate Him from His children today?

Almost as soon as Jesus removed the dividing wall of sin and returned to the right hand of the Father in Heaven, we began to rebuild religious barriers once again! Paul publicly rebuked Peter and Barnabas for resurrecting the old dividing walls of race and religion to separate them from "unclean" Gentile Christians.[11]

As the apostles began to fall in martyrdom and the years progressed, the Church moved away from the freedom Jesus purchased on the cross to embrace the bondage of man's religious agenda and establish man-made "mediators" once again.

Time and again, God intervened to bring correction to the Church by tearing down our self-constructed walls and restoring the things we lost through apathy and apostasy! (Almost as if He had to constantly re-invent the Church.) He brought reformation through Martin Luther and other great reformers; He restored the Scriptures to common men through William Tyndale; and He ignited prayer through the Moravians, revival through the Wesleys, and transformation through countless others who launched hundreds of spiritual renewals, revivals, and "awakenings."

Through it all, God confronted our tendency to drift away from *passion for His presence* toward the relative ease of the lukewarm "religious" life. The Lord has a difficult time "fitting" into the lukewarm churches that have become so common to our generation.[12] No room … no revival. We have learned how to make church comfortable for man, but where is the church that has learned how to make things comfortable for God?

THE PROBLEM IS THAT JESUS WAS "DUAL-NATURED"

Unlike the traveling Tenneys, Jesus did not say, "The Son of Man has nowhere to lay His head"[13] because He had children traveling with Him. He said it because of His *unique nature*. Jesus wasn't saying, "I don't have any friends." Nor was He saying, "I don't have enough money to get a hotel room." He was saying, "I have a hard time finding a place where I fit and where I'm comfortable." The problem is that Jesus was "dual-natured."

If Jesus Christ were purely God, then any legitimate temple of worship would do. If He were just a man, any four-star hotel would do. The problem is that He was both God *and* man. He had to find a refuge that was both a place of worship for divinity and a place of hospitality for humanity. He needed a resting place that would make Him feel at home as Deity, while also caring for His human needs. No dividing wall!

It is one thing to host Him purely as God, or to serve Him purely as a man. It is another thing, however, to host Him as both God and man at the same time!

We think we know what to do for Divinity. Some of us stand and raise our hands in praise and worship while others fall to their knees in repentance and adoration before Him. We know from the Scriptures that you entertain God by worshiping Him. If He were just a man, it would be even easier to show hospitality to Him by meeting the needs with which we are all too familiar. It is the Messianic combination of the two that makes it so difficult for us.

Any study of the Gospel accounts makes it clear that Jesus very often revisited certain places. We understand why He visited Jerusalem so often. It is mentioned by name 821 times in the Bible, and Jesus called it the "city of the great King."[14] We assume that Capernaum is on the list because Jesus did many miracles there and regularly stayed at a house in that city.[15]

WHAT TRANSFORMED MARY AND MARTHA'S HOUSE INTO A HOME?

What about Bethany? Why does it seem like Jesus stayed in Bethany every time He went to Jerusalem? What was so special about that place? I believe Jesus was comfortable at Mary and Martha's house because both His humanity and His divinity were cared for. I think that house became a home to Jesus because *Mary entertained His divinity* and *Martha hosted His humanity.*

This small village is situated on the opposite side of the Mount of Olives from Jerusalem. We know from the Scriptures that Bethany was "a sabbath day's journey"[16] away from Jerusalem, or a distance of about one mile.[17]

This is significant because the Pharisees had a rule that you could walk only so many steps on the sabbath. Anyone who took even one step more had transgressed the Law. (This is the literal origin of the phrase, "Sunday afternoon stroll.")

Jerusalem was a walled city, and the gates of the city were closed at nightfall every day. Jesus didn't mind conducting Kingdom business in Jerusalem, but for some reason, He preferred to leave Jerusalem and stay in Bethany. The village was just within legal "commuting distance" for Jewish travelers anxious to follow the tenets of the Law.

THERE WAS SOMETHING UNIQUE ABOUT THAT HOUSE

Whenever Jesus came to Bethany, He always seemed to gravitate toward Mary and Martha's house.[18] Was it because Martha had the biggest house? We don't know how big her house was; we simply know that she owned one[19] and that there was something about it that made Jesus feel welcome and at home there. There was something unique about that house.

Whatever it was, it caused the same One who said, "The Son of Man has nowhere to lay His head," to say by His actions, "I can lay My head down here. My deity *and* My humanity are at home in this place. I feel welcome and respected here; I feel hosted."

There is an art to hospitality. One Italian restaurant chain I frequent seems to possess a unique understanding of hospitality. When you walk up to the door of these restaurants, you are greeted by a staff member who personally opens the door for you.

Now a "pure business manager" would signal disapproval and say, "You could make better use of that employee who is holding that door open by having him clean tables or wait on customers." I think it is fortunate that a broader thinker prevailed at this restaurant. Someone has learned how to tap the potential available through the art of hospitality. The value and enjoyment of dinner at any restaurant rises when someone goes "the extra mile" to create the right environment of hospitality to make customers feel comfortable.

HE NEEDED TO RECEIVE HOSPITALITY IN TWO REALMS

There was something about the environment at Mary and Martha's house that made Jesus feel especially comfortable there. I'm convinced that the secret to His comfort begins with His dual nature. He was all God, and He was all man. That means He needed to receive hospitality in two realms.

The dual nature of Jesus shows up constantly in the Gospels. One of the clearest examples involves a small fishing boat, a large body of water, and a raging storm:

> *And suddenly a great tempest arose on the sea, so that the boat was covered with the waves.* **But He was asleep.** *Then His disciples came to Him and awoke Him, saying, "Lord, save us! We are perishing!" But He said to them, "Why are you fearful, O you of little faith?" Then He arose and rebuked the winds and the sea, and there was a great calm.*[20]

This description makes most fishermen in my home state of Louisiana[21] immediately think of Lake Pontchartrain, a large lake north of the city of New Orleans. Sports enthusiasts and professional fishermen in other regions such as Wisconsin, Michigan, Illinois, and Ohio can immediately picture the nightmare of being caught in a small craft when one of those incredible winter storms suddenly descends on Lake Superior, Lake Michigan, or Lake Erie.

Even professional fishermen admit that it can get pretty scary riding out a storm in a small boat. Peter, James, and John fished the waters of the Sea of Galilee in boats that weren't large by our standards, but they were large enough to carry Jesus and the 12 disciples.

It appears that at least 7 of the 12 disciples were professional fishermen—men who had fished the waters of the Sea of Galilee all their lives.[22] Jesus was asleep in the bottom of the boat when a storm came up that was so bad that even those seasoned fishermen were convinced they were about to drown!

How bad does a storm have to be for Peter, the bold and self-confident professional fisherman, to say, "I think we're going to die, boys!" *How could Jesus be sound asleep in the middle of such a crisis?*

JESUS' SLUMBER IN THE STORM PROVES HIS HUMANITY

Some would argue that it proves His divinity, reasoning, "He was God; therefore, He could sleep at any point." On the contrary, I think it is proof of His humanity! This incident provides rock-solid proof that the humanity of Jesus could become "bone tired."

On some weekends, I have spoken three times on Saturday and three times on Sunday in up to four different churches or conferences. By the end of the last service late Sunday night, I think I could have slept like a baby if someone would have been kind enough to just lean me up in a corner.

I think Jesus was so tired that He was just passed out in a deep sleep. You have to be pretty tired for a gang of worried sailors to tap you on the shoulder and say, "If You don't wake up, then You're going to drown and not know it!"

When Peter and the others frantically awoke Jesus' exhausted humanity, His divinity stood up and rebuked the wind and the waves. This is a perfect snapshot of the dual nature of Jesus Christ.

HIS HUMANITY DESIRED FRUIT; HIS DIVINITY REBUKED FRUITLESSNESS

In another place, the humanity of Jesus desired food, so He looked for fruit among the green leaves of a fig tree. When His humanity failed to find fruit despite the leafy display typical of healthy and fruit-bearing fig trees, then the divinity of Jesus rebuked the tree and withered it to the root.[23]

The Gospel of Mark implies that the Lord's hunger was out of sync with the usual fruit-bearing season, but the problem really concerned the fig tree's "signal" that it was ready to deliver its fruit early. In any case, it seems that Jesus wanted to drive home a point about "fruitlessness" to His disciples.

Because I am human, food (or the lack of it) is a serious problem for me, especially with my difficult ministry schedule. It is often hard to find any decent food to eat at the late hours I am able to break away for a meal. We finally began to ask our hosts to put us in a "full-service hotel" to help solve our unique problem.

That is when I discovered that some people have a different definition of "full-service hotel" than I do. Most of the places they want to put us are actually fine hotels. They provide clean rooms and a continental breakfast, which is all I would need if I didn't have to contend with such an odd schedule.

The problem is that sometimes I don't get to eat all day because I've flown from morning to night to reach the meeting location. I often shower and rush to the meeting site as soon as I get in, speak that evening, and pray and encourage spiritually hungry people half the night. Finally, I stagger into my hotel room at 11:30 p.m. or later and realize I haven't eaten anything for 12 or more hours. Things can be difficult for me if the hotel doesn't have room service, or if room service ends at 10:00 p.m. because the cooks have gone home.

Many hotels that are not "full-service" don't have a restaurant on the premises. I usually have no car because my hosts graciously offer to pick me up and drop me off at my very nice room. Many times I've had to ask the driver, "Could we swing by a convenience store or grocery store?" Then I take a lonely stroll through the store aisles at 11:30 at night, wondering, *What can I take to the room to eat?*

MANY PEOPLE DON'T UNDERSTAND WHAT A VISITATION FROM GOD REQUIRES

I am sure my hosts loved me, and I know they really did their best to take care of me. The problem was that they just didn't understand. In the same way, there are many people who just don't understand what a visitation from God requires. I would *never* equate a visit by Tommy Tenney with a visitation from God; I'm just saying that people don't understand.

God wants a "full-service hotel." What is a "full-service hotel" for God? It is a place that cares for humanity while it also hosts Divinity.

Whether we like it or not, God will not stay in a motel—He has to have a full-service suite. He won't be satisfied with accommodations featuring adjoining rooms. (He put up with that for more than a millennium when men were permanently separated from Him by the veil of sin and religious division.) He wants nothing less than connecting rooms.

Wherever God and man finally connect, you have the house of Bethany. What started at Bethlehem with a "No Vacancy" sign wound up at Bethany finally with a place for Him to lay His head. Visitation at Jerusalem occurred *because* there was a Bethany.

Endnotes

1. Tommy Tenney, *The God Chasers* (Shippensburg, PA: Destiny Image Publishers, 1998), pp. 17-26.

2. Matthew 8:20 NASB.

3. See Hebrews 13:2.

4. Luke 2:48-50.

5. Luke 2:51a.

6. Ephesians 2:14.

7. Ephesians 2:14, *The Message: New Testament* by Eugene H. Peterson, copyright 1993. Electronic Edition STEP Files copyright 1999, The Learning Company, Inc.

8. I realize that, according to Paul, that dividing wall was "the Law with all of its ordinances," which separated Gentiles from the rich heritage of the Jewish people found in the Law and the Prophets. The Law, however, highlighted the terminal effects of sin and the impossibility of man "earning" his own salvation through works. Even the Jewish people, doing their best to keep the regulations of the Law, could not regain the intimacy of the Garden aside from the grace of God. My point is that the heavenly Father's solution for both problems was to "cut a hole through the dividing wall" by sending His only begotten Son, Jesus Christ, to deliver Jew and Gentile alike through His atoning death on the cross and resurrection from the grave.

9. John 10:7,9b.

10. John 3:16 KJV.

11. See Galatians 2:11-16.

12. See Revelation 3:14-22.

13. Matthew 8:20b.

14. See Matthew 5:35. The number of times Jerusalem is mentioned is cited by the "Search Program" for the keyword "Jerusalem," in "QuickVerse 4.0 Deluxe Bible Reference Collection," by Parsons Technology, One Parsons Drive, P.O. Box 100, Hiawatha, IA 52233-0100.

15. See Mark 2:1. Since the Lord said He didn't have a place to lay His head, we know Jesus did not own this house mentioned in Mark's Gospel. It may have belonged to one of the many disciples who probably lived in Capernaum.

16. Mark 11:1 links Mount Olivet, or the Mount of Olives, with Bethany, and Acts 1:12 says Mount Olivet, the site of the Lord's ascension to Heaven, was "a Sabbath day's journey" away from Jerusalem."

17. Merrill C. Tenney, the former dean of the Graduate School at Wheaton College, said Bethany was "a mile to the eastward on the slope of the

mount of Olives," in his landmark text, *New Testament Survey* (Grand Rapids, MI: Wm. B. Eerdmans Publishing Co., 1961), p. 216.

18. Luke 10:38 says Martha welcomed Jesus "into her house." Some writers think that Martha was a widow who received money and an estate after her husband's death. (A husband is never mentioned in the Gospel accounts.) That would help explain how she had the means to take care of Him (as well as provide the essentials for her younger brother and sister).

19. The Gospels refer to at least three "Marys" whom people often confuse with one another. The Bible also describes an unnamed woman with an unsavory reputation who anointed Jesus with precious ointment, washed His feet with tears, and dried them with her hair. A long-standing theological debate continues about "how many Marys" there are and who did what, when, and where. Some claim there were four Marys; others say there were three Marys (referring to Mary of Nazareth, the mother of Jesus; Mary of Magdala; and Mary of Bethany, while dismissing someone simply called "the other Mary"). My concern in this book has nothing to do with how many Marys there are or how many times Jesus was anointed by women in public. Some people feel, as I do, that it was Mary of Bethany who anointed His feet on one occasion earlier in His ministry *and* anointed His head just before His death. Others say two different Marys or women were involved. Frankly, I don't really care if there were six Marys. In the context of *Chasing God, Serving Man*, I am more concerned with the *attitude* exhibited by each and every Mary or nameless woman who anointed Jesus during a meal. They share the same heart attitude demonstrated by Mary of Bethany when she sat at His feet. It doesn't matter whether or not the Mary at Jesus' feet was the same woman who anointed His head from a broken alabaster box in another Gospel. Why? It is because I am talking about the pure heart of devotion to Him as divinity exhibited by these women. {Theologian Kathleen E. Corley also notes this point in *Private Women, Public Meals: Social Conflict in the Synoptic Tradition* [Peabody, MA: Hendrickson Publishers, 1993], p. 103.) As for the events at Bethany, there may be many Marys, but the Gospel record clearly tells us Jesus stayed at the home of Martha, Lazarus, and their sister Mary.

20. Matthew 8:24-26.

21. For international readers who may be unfamiliar with the geography of North America, Louisiana is located in the southern portion of the United States touching the Gulf of Mexico. It has a strong French cultural background and is known for its great variety of fresh and saltwater fishing.

22. George Cansdale, "Fishing in the Lake of Galilee," an article printed in *Eerdmans' Handbook to the Bible* (Grand Rapids, MI: William B. Eerdmans Publishing Company, 1973), pp. 502-503.

23. Mark 11:13-14,20-21.

Chapter Two

BETHANY OR BETHLEHEM?

Spiritual Segregation Is Wrong!

A little noted Scripture in John 11:1 makes this statement "…Bethany, the town of Mary and her sister Martha." If Bethlehem was infamous for its inhospitable attitude, then Bethany could be famous as a favorite place for Jesus to stay. But it wasn't the quaint streets or the prestigious location that made Bethany a famous favorite. It was Mary and Martha!

I wonder what would have happened if Mary and Martha had not been able to live under the same roof or in the same town? Would Bethany's attractiveness to Jesus have disappeared? When the spiritual is segregated from society, any Bethany can turn into a Bethlehem.

Divide and conquer. Military leaders, emperors, kings, and presidents have followed this simple maxim as a strategy of war for centuries. The adversary of our souls is still using it with great success. A form of "spiritual segregation" is sweeping through the world with incredible force at this writing. It also has infected the Church.

Perhaps you remember your mother or father or a friend's parent taking a stand during your childhood, saying, "Not in my house!" Our heavenly Father is warning the modern Church today:

"I won't live or stay in a place that separates and divides. I won't have it—not in My house."

It is as if God is taking a stand against barriers and separating walls of every kind: "Not in My house!" God Himself is declaring to the blood-bought Church, "I will rip down every dividing wall, because I'm looking for a unified place to dwell."

The pattern of "divide and conquer" sweeping through society and the Church stems from the ancient sin in the Garden of Eden. The serpent initiated his campaign of separation by enticing Eve to seek special status and segregate herself from God's realm by reaching for sin's illicit fruit. Ironically, Adam and Eve created the first "segregated community" when they tried to hide from God after they sinned, covering (or "dividing") their newfound nakedness with fig leaves.[1] The enemy's plan of spiritual segregation succeeded for a time after sin infected mankind, separating us from the Garden of Eden and from God's intimate fellowship.

The effort to separate the spiritual from the secular and remove God from the life of the human race continues today with renewed energy. Spiritual segregation on any level is any effort to lock God out of certain places or out of human activities.

You may often see this statement in this book: "Churches tend to either be spiritually passionate or socially compassionate." Hardly ever is there a balance of both. It's as if satan says, "If I can divide between the two, I can put purpose on pause." This is the essence of spiritual segregation. The drawing of lines between what could be worship creates enmity and animosity between Mary and Martha. If Mary were to leave, the house would turn into a hotel with sterile hospitality. We must not segregate the spiritual from the secular.

SOME WOULD SEGREGATE RIGHTEOUSNESS FROM PUBLIC LIFE

Spiritual segregation takes many forms, but I predict that the next great conflict will come as the forces of immorality wage war against the forces of morality in an effort to *segregate* righteousness from public life.

The process began many years ago, but increasingly we will hear public voices of authority declare, "No, you can't pray in school. No, you can't pray at football games, graduation ceremonies, or on a public park bench. Observe your religious practices all you want to, but do it in private. Keep your faith out of the public arena." *The ultimate goal is to secularize society by making no room for the spiritual in public forums.* The champions of spiritual segregation love to portray righteousness as "old-fashioned, narrow-minded, and hyper-religious." This creates an inhospitable place in human society for divine visitation.

DIVISION GIVES SATAN A "FRESH LEASE ON STRIFE"

Unfortunately, most spiritual segregation actually starts in the Church! The old maxim says, "Divide and conquer." Even though satan is a conquered enemy, we give him a "fresh lease on strife" by *dividing ourselves!*

During the days of the U.S. Civil Rights Movement, Dr. Martin Luther King, Jr. led a non-violent protest march through the city of Birmingham in 1963. The Birmingham police loosed trained attack dogs on the peaceful crowd of men, women, and children, along with tear gas, high-pressure water streams from fire hoses, and nightstick-wielding police officers. Dr. King and other key leaders were arrested and confined in the Birmingham City Jail.[2]

Dr. King described his disappointment over the lukewarm convictions of churches in the South in a historic letter he wrote to his fellow clergy from his Birmingham jail cell:

"I have heard numerous religious leaders of the South call upon their worshippers to comply with a desegregation decision because it is the law, but I have longed to hear white ministers say follow this decree because integration is morally right and the Negro is your brother... In the midst of a mighty struggle to rid our nation of racial and economic injustice, I have heard so many ministers say, "Those are social issues with which the Gospel has no real concern," and I have watched so many churches commit themselves to a completely other-worldly religion *which made a strange distinction between body and soul, the sacred and the secular.*"[3]

"Not only should you worship God on Sunday, but you should serve man on Monday."

Segregation is simply saying, "There is no room for you here."

We have often "ruled" God out of society! (And then wondered why it went so sour.) Whenever spiritual segregation alters a society, it inevitably shows up in the Church in some way. If the racial conflict had its Birmingham, with police dogs and fire hoses enforcing ungodly but "officially sanctioned" racial segregation, then the greater spiritual conflict has its Bethlehem with "No Vacancy" signs and crude accommodations among the beasts of the field.

The forces motivating spiritual segregation in our society aren't content to limit segregation to racial areas. They are determined to declare to people of faith, "We don't have room for you." (It will happen sooner than you think.)

The "Mary/Martha" division of personality and preferences shows up in every level of human society. I have to warn you that if you let her, *Martha will run Mary absolutely out of the picture!* That is her nature. Mary, on the other hand, will impute guilt on Martha because she isn't as "spiritual" as Mary. She will impute guilt on Martha and try to make her feel bad. "Why aren't you down here praying?"

The solution to the crisis may be costly. For every Bethlehem that says there is "No Vacancy" for Him, a Bethany must be created where men and women can prepare a place for Him. Let me say that again in another way: For every Bethlehem that says, "No vacancy— we don't have room for You," there must be a Bethany that becomes a place of hospitality to Divinity and humanity.

If you ever want your city, church, school, or home to have a visitation from God, then somebody has to learn how to host the Holy Ghost. That means you must make accommodations for both man and God. Not only must Mary worship His divinity, but Martha must host His humanity. Not only should you worship God on Sunday, but you should serve man on Monday. Every church house should have both Marys and Marthas. No segregation here! Both must be allowed to thrive. There must be mutual appreciation.

The dual nature of Jesus presents the perfect model for us. He was entertained and hosted in both realms. Christ our head is at the right hand of the Father, but His Body, the Church present and the Church future, lives on earth in physical bodies. He isn't looking for more "Bethlehems" to declare "No Vacancy" when He knocks at the door. He is looking for Bethany, the place of comfort in the house of His friends.

For centuries, church leaders have searched for ways to make people fall in love with the church. Pastors sometimes felt like religious matchmakers, searching for just the right blend of natural and spiritual condiments to create a loyalty to the Church—while nearly forgetting about the God of the Church. The ultimate quest is for *God* and man to get together.

On the other hand, some people fall passionately in love with Him, yet say they can't stand any of their brothers or sisters! "I love God, but I just don't like the Church, and that's fine. It's just God and me in the beauty of God's creation."

I'm sorry, but our heavenly Father doesn't put up with "spiritual sibling rivalry." The writer of the Book of Hebrews said:

And let us consider how we may spur one another on toward love and good deeds. Let us not give up meeting together, as some are in the habit of doing, but let us encourage one another—and all the more as you see the Day approaching.[4]

I don't see any reason why a church cannot be seeker-friendly and Spirit-friendly simultaneously. There is no reason why compassion for man and passion for God cannot coexist.

NOTHING TAKES THE PLACE OF FAMILY RELATIONSHIPS IN THE BODY

It is difficult to consider, encourage, and spur one another "toward love and good deeds" when we are busy "doing our own thing with God" while out in a wheat field or perched on a mountaintop somewhere. Those places provide wonderful opportunities to consider God's wonder and praise His name, but they cannot and will not take the place of the family relationships in the Body of Christ.

The way some people act in church often reminds me of the time my sister and I took a long trip with my father in his car. Long earthly trips can get rather "interesting." My sister and I used to draw an imaginary line down the middle of the backseat of the car and say, "This is my side; that's your side. Don't cross the line."

On good days, we lasted maybe two hours on an eight-hour trip before erupting in a bout of sibling rivalry. "Dad, her foot is on my side! No, Dad, his hand is over here." We blindly continued our family feud with verbal claims and counterclaims, "He's on my side," and "No, she's on my side," with no understanding that neither one of us had claim on the backseat or on the car—it was Dad's car. Then illumination would come with a single sentence from my father: "Don't make me have to stop this car." Suddenly we remembered who really owned the car and what happened when his "passengers" failed to listen to his warning.

Nothing makes a father any sadder than to see his children refusing to live together in peace in the same house. Consider the tension we create for our heavenly Father when we choose to constantly be at war with one another. He loves all of us, and He is asking us, "Can't we all just get along?"

IT REALLY ISN'T OUR CHURCH—IT'S HIS

As church people, we like to draw artificial lines of division and erect man-made barriers between us. We like to tell one another in superior tones reminiscent of our backseat territorial battles, "I'm doing this, but she's doing that, and it isn't her area." Somehow, it never seems to dawn on us that it isn't our church—it's His.

I wonder how many times the Father has had to warn His battling children:

> "Don't make Me have to stop My purposes! Children, you are arguing over something that doesn't even belong to you. You have no right to argue over positions, power, or politics in the Church—it isn't yours. It's Mine! It's not 'your side'; it is My family. Don't worry about what your brother and sister are doing—work out your own salvation with fear and trembling. Whether you serve behind the pulpit, behind the nursery door, or behind a broom on Saturday night, it is all precious to Me."

Unity is a hot topic in the Church right now, partly because it is God's heart and partly because we have made such a mess of things by confusing "unity in mind and spirit" with "uniformity in mind and flesh." I dealt with this critical topic in my book, *God's Dream Team*:

> The enemy offers, in clever disguise, false unity. It's man-made bricks. It is a unity built on uniformity, born of control and oblivious to the truth. ***Ecumenicalism has offered diluted doctrine and created false unity.*** The ecumenical movement is a coming together based on finding and maintaining our lowest common denominator—not our highest calling and purpose...
>
> ...Perhaps what the Church needs to sign is a "Declaration of Dependence"—we totally depend on each other and absolutely depend on Him! What some people call "independent" means granting self-expression to a group of undisciplined individuals.[5]

There is a clear and critical difference between biblical unity and man-made uniformity. We must understand that God really values the differences, characteristics, and service of both Mary and Martha.

CAUGHT IN THE MIDDLE BETWEEN MARY AND MARTHA

Have you ever found yourself caught between some of your "Martha friends" and your "Mary friends"? Some of my good friends have a standard reaction whenever I talk about some other friends with a different view of the Christian life. The first group of friends might say, "Well, he's just a mystic." I might reply to them, "That's odd. I thought he was a Christian...."

When I'm among the second group of friends and mention someone in the first group who is passionate about social outreach to the poor and downtrodden in inner cities, they might comment, "Well, yeah, that's all well and good, but he doesn't really understand things of the Spirit."

I feel compelled to embrace both "sides" of my Christian family. We have a God-ordained mandate to stand in the gap and become a bridge of compassionate understanding between them. That only happens when we begin to see that God values both viewpoints— He just longs to see them work together.

IS "MIDNIGHT OIL" THE SAME AS ANOINTING OIL?

It is obvious to us that Mary loved Jesus; she set the supreme example of loving worship when she broke her costly alabaster box of perfume to anoint Him for His death. However, we must ask ourselves if brokenness is only exemplified by breaking an alabaster box and pouring out anointing oil. Is it possible that brokenness also can be exemplified by burning the "midnight oil" and staying up all night before the Passover to prepare the last supper for Him? Can "burning-heart" service be "broken-willed" worship? Could it be that "someone's in the kitchen" with Martha?

Spiritual segregation has no place in God's purposes or in the life of any local church. Mary and Martha must not only live in the *same neighborhood*, they must live in the *same house!* No spiritual segregation, no prideful prejudice.

If we can't sit together on earth, will we dwell together in Heaven?

Broken relationships in the Body of Christ are the New Testament equivalent of human sacrifice. If we feel we have to break relationships with our brethren, then that also means we feel we need to sacrifice Jesus Christ on the altar of our own opinion. It is His Body and heart we are dismembering. We must overcome that to create unity in the Body. I think this is what is meant by "discerning the Body."[6]

Are We a Light of Divine Hope on the Hill of Humanity?

The efforts of individuals, institutions, and governments to enforce "spiritual segregation" arose during an era when the lukewarm Church wasn't really functioning as the genuine Church. We were focused on ourselves, and we were constantly occupied with "bickering in the backseat of Daddy's car" instead of being a light of divine hope on the hill of humanity.

I'm convinced that once the members of Christ's Body come to terms with one another and begin to live in peace and unity, then we will "be about our Father's business." It is impossible for the forces of darkness to extinguish or dim the light of the Church when she is worshiping, functioning, and serving to her full supernatural potential in God's purposes!

Our Father is looking for a house or tabernacle to *live* in, not simply to *visit*. When God is in the house, when Divinity is in habitation with His human family, we will have reached the zenith of true spiritual "warfare." The truth of God's promise through John will be clear:

*You are of God, little children, and have overcome them, because **He who is in you** is greater than he who is in the world.*[7]

At that point, the only "spiritual segregation" permitted will be the sovereign work of God Himself, as He divides the true sheep from the goats and wolves.[8]

Endnotes

1. See Genesis 3:7.

2. This is a description of the violent mistreatment of a group of predominately African-American civil rights demonstrators who were led by the late Dr. Martin Luther King, Jr. in a peaceful foot march through Birmingham, Alabama. The effort of the city leaders to stop the procession backfired when the attacks made the national news. Birmingham became the rallying cry of the growing civil rights movement, and it helped sway many non-black Americans and national leaders to the side of the protestors.

3. This quote is excerpted from the historic "Letter From Birmingham City Jail" written by Dr. Martin Luther King, Jr. to appeal to his fellow clergy in that city. Reproduced from a citation on the University of Western Michigan Political Science Internet site: www.wmich.edu/politics/mlk. Accessed 3/19/2001. Emphasis mine.

4. Hebrews 10:24-25 NIV.

5. Tommy Tenney, *God's Dream Team: A Call to Unity* (Ventura, CA: Regal Books, a division of Gospel Light; 1999), Chapter 3, "Unity, Not Conformity," pp. 54-55.

6. Ibid, p. 57.

7. 1 John 4:4.

8. See Matthew 7:15-23; 25:31-46.

Chapter Three

WHY AREN'T YOU LIKE ME?

Will Mary and Martha Ever Get Along?

Every year I minister in hundreds of churches and conferences in North America and around the world. One thing I've noticed that never seems to vary from meeting to meeting or even from culture to culture is that people see things *differently*.

When I talk to people about what happened in a meeting, I am always amazed at the different perceptions they share with me. Very often, I hear totally different reports from two people who sat beside each other in the same service!

One person might say, "That was the worst service I've ever attended. I didn't understand a thing they were saying, and all they wanted to do was stand up for hours and sing songs I don't know and don't care about learning. They just cried and talked to God the whole night, and nobody talked to me. It seemed to bless everybody else, but it didn't do a thing for me."

If you talk to someone who sat right beside the first person during the same service, he might grin from ear to ear and say, "That was the most incredible service I've ever attended! The presence of God was so thick in the room that you could feel it. I can't remember crying so hard before. Best of all, I felt like a new person when it was all over."

There is such a dichotomy between the two witnesses that you have to wonder if they were really talking about the same meeting or two entirely different events. How can that be? They both attended the same meeting, but they perceived it from two radically different viewpoints.

Mary and Martha of Bethany provide the perfect model for these viewpoints. *Martha* majors on the practical and minors on the spiritual. *Mary* seems to focus almost exclusively on the spiritual realm while downplaying or nearly overlooking the practical details of life and Christian service.

DISSECTING THE DICHOTOMY BETWEEN MARY AND MARTHA

One of the biggest problems we face in the Church is that our Marys and Marthas just can't seem to get along. But before we can propose solutions to the problem, we must dissect the dichotomy between Mary and Martha. Wisdom for every problem comes through prayer, diligent thought, and the proper application of God's principles in life.

We usually find Marys on their knees before the Lord. Their chief distinguishing mark is the position of their heart. At Martha's house, we see Mary's telltale posture of worship and adoration at the feet of Jesus. The same thing happens later during the meal held at the house of Simon the leper in Bethany. Each time she endured criticism and outcry to assume her position and pour out her gift to the Lord.[1]

What about Martha? Many people read about Martha serving in the kitchen and announce with great authority, "Well, Jesus didn't really like Martha; He only liked Mary." If you examine the Scriptures, you'll discover that just isn't true. John tells us immediately after Jesus received a message that Lazarus was sick, "Now Jesus *loved Martha* and her sister and Lazarus."[2] In that moment of crisis, Jesus' mind was on Martha. Mary isn't even mentioned by name in this sentence.

Many Bible students and teachers criticize Martha's fixation with "dirty dishes" and the narrow priorities of the kitchen. For similar reasons, many mothers today are cautioned by the modern proverb, "Dirty dishes can be washed later, but little children can only be held for so long." However, Martha's biggest problem wasn't a dirty kitchen, unwashed vegetables, or interrupted meal preparations—*it was her attitude toward Mary.*

MODERN MARTHAS WRESTLE WITH ATTITUDES ABOUT MODERN MARYS

Modern-day Marthas face the same problem. Their "cross" in life has more to do with their attitudes toward "modern-day Marys" than anything else in the local church. Perhaps she felt that Mary's devotion had gone over the line of reason into doting on Jesus. Surely Jesus, the wise Teacher, would understand her position as chief cook and elder sister in the household. The truth is that Jesus did understand her position; He just didn't accept her nearsighted priority system.

Whenever Jesus came to Bethany and entered the house of Mary and Martha, they didn't know whether it was time to feed His humanity or worship His divinity. Sometimes He just wanted "biscuits and gravy"; at other times He was to be received as Divinity. Sometimes Martha met the Son of Man's most urgent need by providing home-cooked food, comfortable accommodations, and an orderly and peaceful home environment for His humanity. At other times the Son of God most longed for the ministry of Mary, who had a gift for entertaining His divinity.

For this reason, the house of Mary and Martha offers us a unique perspective of how ordinary people in our day can successfully entertain the dual-natured Risen Christ: We worship and "chase" the divinity of His manifested presence, and we serve the humanity of His Body on earth.

Both of these sisters loved Jesus, and they both appreciated His presence and His friendship. Yet, there were times when they didn't

get along. It is virtually impossible to entertain Divinity and humanity at the same time if Mary and Martha refuse to work together in
unity. Why is there such tension between them? Perhaps we can find
the key in the conflict Jesus confronted at Martha's house.

> *Now it happened as they went that He entered a certain village;*
> *and a certain woman named Martha welcomed Him into her house.*
> *And she had a sister called Mary, who also sat at Jesus' feet and*
> *heard His word. But Martha was distracted with much serving,*
> *and she approached Him and said, "Lord, do You not care that my*
> *sister has left me to serve alone? Therefore tell her to help me."*[3]

THESE OPPOSITES REPEL ONE ANOTHER

Mary and Martha are more than simply "different." Left to themselves, these two opposites *repel* one another! When that happens, it
is difficult to create the environment that drew Jesus to Bethany time
and again.

In the incident described by Luke, Jesus became the Divine
Mediator who brought balance and peace to two radically different
branches of humanity represented in Martha and Mary. The Lord
made it clear that He valued the service of both of Lazarus' sisters,
but from that moment on, that house and city was known as the
home of Mary and Martha. Why?

Although the Lord honors and appreciates our "Martha ministry" to humanity, our *eternal* destiny culminates in an everlasting
"Mary ministry" to Divinity. As long as Mary and Martha live
together in one house, there is bound to be a dynamic tension
between the two. It takes the mediation of Jesus Christ to bring rec-
onciliation in a house occupied by such opposites.

As any pastor will quickly confirm, the Marthas in the typical local
church are usually wondering, "Why in the world doesn't 'that Mary'
get over here and help me in this kitchen? If she wants to be so spiritual, then she needs to drag herself over here and help me feed these
hungry folk and clothe the naked. If she was really all that spiritual, she

would get up off the floor and stop all that boo-hooing and crying long enough to do something that really helps hurting people."

The Marys in the church are saying to themselves, "I wish 'that Martha' would just forget about all that cooking. She should know that when you're really spiritual, you don't have to eat. I wish she would get out of that kitchen and come over here. She needs to lose the apron and get on her knees before Jesus. What she needs is some old-fashioned 'praying through' time in God's presence. That would take care of her unspiritual devotion to the works of her hands."

The truth is that it takes *both ministries* to make Jesus feel genuinely comfortable in the house. He is risen, yet He still dwells among us and even manifests His "concentrated" presence at times. He is our Head, and we, as the Church, are His earthly Body. Just as it was difficult for Him to find a resting place during His earthly ministry because He was both God and man, so in our day He still searches for a place that ministers to both Divinity and humanity with equal ease and hospitality.

"Perhaps one of the greatest obstacles to His habitation among us is that very seldom can the Marys and Marthas in the Church live at peace in the same house."

Perhaps one of the greatest obstacles to His habitation among us is that very seldom can the Marys and Marthas in the Church live at peace in the same house.

One of the problems with modern Marys is that they are tempted to pretend that Jesus' manifest presence is *always* in the house. The truth is that He is not always there in the sense of His *manifest presence*.

AM I SPIRITUALLY DEAD, OR ARE THEY SEEING SOMETHING?

Nothing frustrates me more than the people who say, "Oh, God is here! Look, God is there!" (when He really isn't any more present

"there" than He is "here"). I just want to know, "Where?" Am I spiritually dead, or are they seeing something that isn't really there? I
am sure that sometimes people really are sensing His manifest presence, and when I ask them, "Where?" I literally want directions and
guidance to find Him. "Where? Tell me! I want to feel Him; I want
to know Him." Like the Greek God Chasers in John's Gospel, I
humbly say, "Sir, Ma'am, I want to *see* Jesus."[4]

Mary's great gift was her single-minded devotion to the Master
when He was in the house; yet, modern Marys suffer from our generation's sad satisfaction with second-best. As I noted in *God's
Favorite House*:

> The Bride of Christ has grown accustomed to living in the King's
> house *in His absence*. If she would return to the passion and
> hunger of her first love, she would never be so content unless the
> King Himself were present with her in the house.[5]

Once a "modern Mary" tastes the "real thing" of God's manifest
presence, she enters her greatest place of anointing and service to the
Lord. In His absence, "prostrate Marys" can cause great damage
through misplaced spiritual zeal if they promote *false* revival. The
greatest damage occurs when they make "modern Marthas" in the
local church feel guilty because they don't perceive Him and have
trouble leaving their places of preparation and service to the humanity in the house.

WE NEED THE SPIRITUAL SERVICE
OF PRACTICAL MARTHAS

Mary's greatest weakness was, perhaps, her dislike or lack of
appreciation for Martha's vital role in ministering to the humanity of
Jesus (and of the ministry of "modern Marthas" to the humanity for
whom Jesus manifests His presence). I have a good friend who is an
ardent student of the Christian mystics who blazed the trail of God
chasing in generations gone by. He told me a story from the life of a

"Desert Father" named Abba Silvanus that clearly demonstrates the need for the spiritual service of practical "Marthas":

> A brother went to see Abba Silvanus on the mountain of Sinai. When he saw the brothers working hard, he said to the old man, "Do not labor for the food which perishes (John 6:27). Mary has chosen the good portion (Luke 10:42)."
>
> The old man said to his disciple, "Zacharias, give the brother a book and put [him] in a cell without anything else." So, when the ninth hour came the visitor watched the door expecting someone would be sent to call him to the meal.
>
> When no one called him he got up, went to find the old man and said to him, "Have the brothers not eaten today?" The old man replied that they had. Then he said, "Why did you not call me?" The old man said to him, "Because you are a spiritual man and do not need that kind of food. We, being carnal, want to eat, and that is why we work. But you have chosen the good portion and read the whole day long and you do not want to eat carnal food."
>
> When he heard these words the brother made a prostration saying, "Forgive me, Abba." The old man said to him, "Mary needs Martha. It is really thanks to Martha that Mary is praised."[6]

WHO DO WE NEED THE MOST: VISIONARY OR IMPLEMENTER?

Mary and Martha find it difficult to get along because they view the world from totally different places. Faced with a challenge, Mary would probably say, "Whatever it takes," while Martha would say, "What would it take?"

Mary is a visionary, and Martha is a planner and implementer. Mary is the eternal idealist, and Martha is the earthy realist. Frankly, we need both anointings to build a house suitable for lasting Divine habitation. If you doubt this, ask yourself this question: "Who do I need the most: visionary or implementer?" No matter what choice you make, no project, dream, or vision will come to pass without the full operation and cooperation of people from both "sides" of the process.

It you told a contractor that you wanted a three-story house and then said, "This is what I want. Now I've only allotted enough resources for either an architect or a carpentry crew. Choose which one you want, and then tell me how long it will take to complete my building." The contractor would probably shake his head and say good-bye at that point.

Our challenge is to follow in the footsteps of Jesus and help Martha understand Mary's position (and vice versa). It seems like Jesus was constantly reminding the disciples, the Pharisees and lawyers, and everyday people like Mary and Martha: "Yes, you are My child, but this one is also My child, although he is different from you."

There is another aspect of the Christian life that brings out our differences as well. It costs each of us something to be Jesus' friend because it requires us to operate on His "time clock" and according to His purposes, not ours.[7] If you were to ask Lazarus, the brother of Mary and Martha, "Lazarus, what was it like, being raised from the dead?" He would probably say, "Oh, that was great! It was that 'dying part' that wasn't so cool."[8]

GOD MAY SACRIFICE YOUR TEMPORARY CONVENIENCE FOR ETERNAL PURPOSES

Lazarus would tell you that God may sacrifice your short-term convenience or comfort for the sake of His eternal purposes. (He also would tell you it is always worth it in the end.) Martha discovered on one particular day when Jesus came to her house that her elaborate plans to prepare a four-course meal with all the trimmings had to be set aside. Mary (being Mary) knew instinctively what Martha had to learn the hard way: They were in God's time zone, and everything they'd planned in their time zone was to be suspended for a while.

Both sisters would face a far more difficult lesson in the timing and priorities of God when Lazarus fell sick and died. By their timetable, Jesus should have suspended all Kingdom operations, postponed the Father's plans, dropped everything else, and rushed to Bethany to heal their brother. After all, wasn't Lazarus the Lord's friend? It was unthinkable that the same Teacher and Friend who stayed in their home and ate at their family table would delay His coming even one day. It was beyond their (and our) comprehension that by His absence He would let Lazarus suffer. It would almost be more than they could bear to know that Jesus heard the news but still tarried until days after the burial.[9]

MARTHA TOOK MATTERS INTO HER OWN HANDS

When Jesus finally appeared on the road that led into Bethany, Martha couldn't wait—she took matters in her own hands and left the ongoing funeral wake to meet Jesus on the road even before He entered Bethany.

Mary chose not to leave the house of her mourning, refusing for the moment even to seek the Master's hand in her grief. Perhaps she felt the pain too deeply, or perhaps she was too disappointed in the Lord's delay to celebrate the Lord's return once her brother was in the grave. Jesus received two different receptions from the sisters of Bethany. They shared some common words, but they were present- ed from two entirely different positions of petition:

Now Martha, as soon as she heard that Jesus was coming, went and met Him, but Mary was sitting in the house. Now Martha said to Jesus, "Lord, if You had been here, my brother would not have died. But even now I know that whatever You ask of God, God will give You." Jesus said to her, "Your brother will rise again." Martha said to Him, "I know that he will rise again in the resurrection at the last day." Jesus said to her, "I am the resurrec- tion and the life. He who believes in Me, though he may die, he shall live. And whoever lives and believes in Me shall never die. Do you believe this?" She said to Him, "Yes, Lord, I believe that

*You are the Christ, the Son of God, who is to come into the world."
And when she had said these things, she went her way and secretly called Mary her sister, saying, "The Teacher has come and is
calling for you."*[10]

JESUS IGNORES OUR PRESUMPTIONS
TO MINISTER TO OUR REAL NEED

Martha intercepted Jesus even before He reached Bethany. (This
seems typical of all "action-oriented Marthas.") Instead of greeting
Him in great relief or laying her burdens at His feet, she bypassed all
of the expected protocols of politeness to boldly confront Him over
what she clearly implied was an error in judgment or personal priorities.[11] Jesus demonstrated His grace and mercy toward her and
ignored her insulting presumptions to minister to her real need. I'm
thankful that in our day, He still ignores our presumptions to minister to our real need.

Jesus knew that Martha needed to see past the humanity she
served so faithfully to fully perceive and receive His divinity. He
told her, "I am the resurrection and the life," and then asked if she
believed it. At that point Martha made a confession of faith very similar to the confession made by Peter the disciple: "Yes, Lord, I believe
that You are the Christ, the Son of God, who is to come into the
world."[12]

If the manifest presence of God comes to your "house" in true
revival and resurrection power, don't be surprised if some people
are so hurt or upset with Him that they won't even come out to meet
Him! (They are usually angry or hurt because He hasn't come *when*
they wanted or *where* they expected. Some people get outraged
because He didn't come in the *way* they expected Him to come.)

*...[Martha] secretly called Mary her sister, saying, "The Teach-
er has come and is calling for you." As soon as she heard that,
she arose quickly and came to Him....in the place where Martha
met Him. Then the Jews who were with her in the house, and*

comforting her, when they saw that Mary rose up quickly and went out, followed her, saying, "She is going to the tomb to weep there." Then, when Mary came where Jesus was, and saw Him, she fell down at His feet, saying to Him, "Lord, if You had been here, my brother would not have died." Therefore, when Jesus saw her weeping, and the Jews who came with her weeping, He groaned in the spirit and was troubled.[13]

When Mary finally rose from her grief to meet the Prince of Peace, she said the same words Martha did—but *first she fell down at His feet in humble brokenness*. The results were dramatically different.

Jesus didn't bother to strengthen Mary's faith or correct her theology as He did with Martha. Perhaps it was because Mary's faith was rooted in her relationship with His divinity rather than in her friendship with His humanity. In any case, He could do nothing about the pain she had already suffered; it was necessary if He was to reveal the Father's resurrection power again in advance of the cross.

"Martha stood before Him in bold confrontation. Mary fell down at His feet in humble brokenness."

Mary didn't ask Him for anything; she just collapsed at His feet and bared her broken heart. When confronted by Mary's tears and brokenness, Jesus again revealed His *humanity* when He wept openly before friends, enemies, and strangers. Then He rose in His *divinity* and set out to upend the natural laws of death and decay and raise Mary and Martha's dead brother.

I'm convinced that Mary had a Spirit-birthed premonition in her heart that something "big" was about to happen that would change their lives forever. (She had no clue just how much life would change.) In fact, Mary may have been the only one out of the hundreds of people around Jesus who "caught" the hints He dropped about His impending death. Evidently none of the disciples caught on until the night He was arrested, or even later.[14]

MARY AND MARTHA ARE DIFFERENT, BUT WE NEED THEM BOTH

Mary leaned toward the place of adoration and faith; Martha had a natural preference for the place of service or works of faith. Yes, Mary and Martha are different, but we need them both. The Word says, "Faith without works is dead."[15] Martha would instinctively labor to clothe the naked, but we suspect that Mary might have been tempted to just pray for the naked (and close her eyes to avoid being distracted by their nakedness).

The Lord helped me see another difference between Mary and Martha during a ministry trip to Senegal in West Africa. Senegal is situated in a very arid desert region near the edge of Africa's great Sahara Desert. One of my missionary hosts said, "We have to schedule our baptisms because we have to bring water with us. There is never enough water in a village to waste for baptism."

When it is time to conduct water baptisms, they put a 55-gallon drum of water in the back of a pickup truck and drive out to the villages. Anyone who wants to be baptized must climb down into the drum, and when it is time to go under the water, the minister kind of pushes him under the surface, and he pops back up like a jack-in-the-box.

I began to think about it in the context of Mary and Martha and came to some interesting conclusions. If you are a modern Mary, you would take the water out to the villages exactly as the missionaries do right now. Of course, there isn't any extra water available for them to drink, but baptism into the Lord is the main focus, after all.

If you are a modern Martha, you probably would be more concerned about transporting pure water to those villages so the people would have something to drink in that arid land.

ARRANGE A MARRIAGE OF MARY AND MARTHA'S PLANS

I decided that if it was up to me, I'd arrange a marriage of Mary and Martha's plans. It seemed logical to drive that pickup truck to the village with the 55-gallon drum filled with water. After everyone had been baptized and the last person had bobbed to the top, I would have the people remove the 55-gallon drum and build a fire under it. After the water has boiled long enough to purify it, it should be poured through a clean and sterile straining cloth into smaller containers and distributed as drinking water. In this way, the Church is blessed in obedience to God's ordinance of water baptism, and the Church becomes a blessing to humanity at the same time.

There is a certain dynamic tension between Mary and Martha, and the list of "opposites" we could compile is seemingly endless. However, I'm convinced that Jesus always meets us in the center of that relational dynamic. Mary and Martha don't always get along, but God refuses to let it stay that way. He is happiest when both Mary and Martha are in the house and working together in harmony, joining their differences together at His feet.

Endnotes

1. See Luke 10:38-40 and John 12:1-8, respectively.

2. John 11:5.

3. Luke 10:38-40.

4. See John 12:20-21.

5. Tommy Tenney, *God's Favorite House* (Shippensburg, PA: Fresh Bread, an imprint of Destiny Image Publishers, 1999), quoted from Chapter 2, "False Finish Lines and Scented Doorknobs," p. 18.

6. My friend, Don L. Milam, Jr., author of *The Lost Passions of Jesus* (Shippensburg, PA: Mercy Place, an imprint of Destiny Image Publishers, 1999), first sent me a copy of this story. We also found it on the "Inner Light Productions" website at www.innerlightproductions.com/thoughts/feb2298.htm. This

excerpt was cited from Benedicta Ward's book, *The Desert Christian* (New York: MacMillan, 1975), p. 223.

7. Some readers may think it impertinent to speak of being a "friend" to Jesus. For many centuries, this was the official dogma of many church organizations. Again, we should consult the Scriptures as the final authority in all matters. Jesus spoke specifically to His disciples concerning His friendship with mankind in John 15:14-16. Jesus also spoke to His disciples and referred to Lazarus as "our friend" in John 11:11.

8. This fictional exchange with Lazarus also appears in my book, *The God Catchers* (Nashville, TN: Thomas Nelson Publishers, 2000), p. 86.

9. See John 11:1-17.

10. John 11:20-28.

11. The very next verse makes us suspect that Martha reverted to her familiar "take charge" methods when she *secretly* sent what may have been a *fabricated lie* to Mary. (John never said that Jesus asked for Mary, and it is unlikely he would omit such a detail.)

12. John 11:27. Compare this with the confession of another "Martha" named Peter, who also received a revelation of Christ's divinity in Matthew 16:16.

13. John 11:28-33.

14. Despite the many advance warnings Jesus gave them about His impending death and resurrection on the third day, the disciples and the majority of the people who followed Jesus to the end were in shock when it came to pass. When Mary Magdalene and other witnesses told the disciples about the tomb and the angels, the Bible says, "And their words seemed to them like idle tales, and they did not believe them" (Lk. 24:11). The two men on the road to Emmaus were so discouraged when Jesus died without freeing Israel from Rome's tyranny that they doubted His resurrection (see Luke 24:13-33).

15. James 2:20b.

Chapter Four

LEAVE ME ALONE…

Let Mary Be Mary; Let Martha Be Martha

The last time I checked, God planned for us to be conformed to only one image—and it wasn't "our own" image. He didn't authorize us to conform *other people* to our own image either, but we like the idea so much that many of us adopted it as our own idea of godly "ministry."

Like so many bridegrooms before me, I married my wife thinking, "She is a great girl. By the time I finish training her, she's going to be incredible." (Once you stop snickering, you could probably finish this story for me.)

I'm not sure who has been "trained" now, but neither one of us would want to start over. I often tell people in our meetings, "I'm thoroughly housebroken and totally trained. In fact, I know exactly what it means when my wife calls me 'handsome.' It means 'hand some over.'" (I'll let you figure out "who trained who.")

I presumptuously imagined that I could "train" my wife to be logical and analytical—like me, of course. I soon realized that my efforts to conform her "to my own image" only raised her frustration level (and mine as well).

It took me many years to realize that my wife is different from me for a very good reason. It dawned on me that it was unreasonable to think she would be "better" if she somehow conformed to my image of what is best and what isn't. From that point on, our marriage relationship became a whole lot more interesting and a lot less frustrating for both of us.

We discovered several years ago that our eldest daughter thinks like me more than my wife does. For that reason, it isn't unusual for staff members to take their questions to my daughter when I am out of the country or otherwise unreachable. They've learned that she can generally give them a clue about how I'd approach their problem if I were there.

HER WAY OF THINKING AND MINE ARE DIFFERENT

Now if my staff members simply need an authoritative answer, they pose the same question to my wife. She usually can answer their questions just as well and as accurately as I can. The difference is that she couldn't tell them *how* she arrived at that answer, let alone tell them how I would do it. Why? Her way of thinking and mine are *Different* (yes, with a capital "D").

If we agreed to drive across town in separate cars, my wife would go one way and I would another. We would both wind up at the same place, but I could tell you why I took the specific route I chose. My wife might even reach the place quicker than I would, but she probably couldn't explain why she took one road instead of another. She would tell you matter-of-factly, "I don't know; it's just what I always do." (I don't want to get in trouble here, but that is just the way it is.) Is my way better? No, it is simply the way I prefer.

Nothing will create more confusion in your life, in your church, or in your home than misguided efforts to force Marthas to become Marys or to force Marys to function like Marthas. It doesn't work.

If you manage to pull a Martha away from her work long enough to sit down "at the feet of Jesus" for an extended period, she would enjoy it for a while (after all, Marthas love Jesus too). Before long, however, though Martha's body might be in a posture of prayer, her thoughts would be wandering back to the dirty dishes in the sink. She will be thinking about all the things that must be done in the house to properly host the Lord and any guests who come to see Him. It is just the way she is.

IT IS PART OF HER "SPIRITUAL DNA"

You can take Martha out of the soup kitchens on skid row, but you will never take away her love and longing to serve others. It is part of her "spiritual DNA."

If you coax Mary into the kitchen and try to make her into a Martha, it won't be long before she is staring out of the window or glancing over her shoulder toward her favorite place of prayer and encounter, saying, "I wish I could be in there...." You're not going to change that.

You can take Mary out of her prayer closet or place of worship, but you will never be able to remove prayer and worship from Mary's heart and personality. Again, it is part of her "spiritual DNA."

If we can't change others to make them think exactly the way we do, then what is the real meaning of unity? Why is it so important for us to value the gifts and abilities God placed in each one of us? I noted in my book on biblical unity, *God's Dream Team*:

> Unity is not the total absence of conflict. That might be uni-formity. Unity is agreeing with your adversary while you are walking together.[1] *Conciliation is not compromise.* We need a spirit of reconciliation to bring us to the point of unity. We need it in our hearts and in our homes. We need it among friends and fellow laborers. We need it everywhere. Satan is sowing seeds of division at every possible junction. *We don't need relationship breakers; we need relationship menders.*[2]

PREEMPTIVE PREPARATION
MAY PRECIPITATE VISITATION

Sometimes Martha's "preemptive preparation" for God's humanity creates the perfect atmosphere for a visitation by Divinity. The Bible says:

> *Now it happened as they went that He entered a certain village; and a certain woman named **Martha welcomed Him** into her house. And she had a sister called Mary, who also sat at Jesus' feet and heard His word.*[3]

The only reason Mary had the opportunity to sit at the feet of Jesus in the living room was because Martha invited Jesus into the house and labored in the kitchen to prepare Him a meal. *Martha's ministry of hospitality to the Lord literally created the platform for Mary's ministry of worship!* Somehow I don't believe things have changed much today. It is time to let Mary be Mary, and let Martha be Martha. Then the complete kingdom purpose is accomplished.

Martha's practice of "preemptive preparation" stands out as unique in the New Testament, but it isn't new. She wasn't the first woman who made special preparations to host God's man in her home. A notable woman in a town called "Rest" (the literal meaning of *Shunem*) actually "fastened onto" the prophet Elisha and strongly persuaded him to eat a meal in her home.[4]

This woman didn't stop there. She quickly moved to the next step of preemptive preparation by persuading her husband to build a special prophet's chamber for the man of God.

"Honey, have you noticed that bald-headed prophet who passes by here all the time? Unless I'm totally wrong, he doesn't seem to have a place to stay."

"Yes, and so...?"

"...So, I have an idea. I think we need to build a small guest room for him on the side of the house. You know, with a prophet-sized bed and a nice table and chair so he can prepare his messages there. And make sure you put in some good olive oil lighting...I think he gets in late at night after some of those prophetic encounters...."

THE SHUNAMMITE WOMAN HAD MARY'S HEART AND MARTHA'S ABILITY

What does this have to do with Mary and Martha? How does it apply to the average local church setting? The Shunammite woman had the heart of Mary when it came to valuing the prophetic presence of God represented by Elisha, yet she also had Martha's practical ability of preemptive preparation for visitation. It takes both kinds of anointing to perceive and anticipate His coming and prepare for it in practical ways.

"Everybody wants to profit from the prophet, but no one wants to pay his hotel bill!"

It is fine for a local church to build an elaborate house and feast on favorite "family foods" (ministry programs). It is all right to have a preferred music collection, where you say, "We're going to sing this song first, then we'll have a solo during the offering, and follow up with these three songs in this key." However, if you want the presence of God to stop and stay at the house, you will have to prepare Him a place.

Whenever the Dove, the Holy Spirit, flies by, you must create the place for Him to land. Suspend your own agenda to attend to the needs of Divinity. That is how you "build a prophet's chamber."

Every time I speak on this topic or hear someone minister on this passage, I see a lot of people nodding their heads in approval. That is all well and good, but I've noticed that everybody wants to profit from the prophet, but no one wants to pay his hotel bill! The Shunammite woman was willing to pay the price to go beyond the "one-day stay" over a shared loaf of bread. She and her husband invested effort and finances to create an environment for the prophet to *stay* as a permanent invited guest.

Like Martha hundreds of years later, the woman of Shunem prepared ahead of time to host God's anointing. As a result, he spoke into her life on behalf of God, bringing her a son in her old age, and later on he brought new life to that son after the child died prematurely. She made her bed…and her son had to lie on it in death. What if there had been no prepared place? Her future would have been aborted.

These two women blazed a trail of "preemptive preparation" by serving the humanity carrying the anointing of divinity. For both of these God Chasers, the statement rings true: The habitation they prepared for God's servant produced resurrection life when death knocked at the family door.[5]

How can we compare Martha with Mary? Someone said, "Martha is the St. Peter, Mary the St. John of [the fairer] sex."[6]

History tells us that most churches have found it easier to understand Marthas than Marys. As the intimate knowledge of Jesus Christ waned and the love of man's knowledge took its place, darkness moved in on the Church. Politics and power became the focal point of many religious leaders, rather than intimacy and submission to the will of God. Nevertheless, every generation has had its Marys, its God Chasers who braved persecution, misunderstanding, and possible death to pursue Him.

THE MORE THE CHURCH LOST ITS SALT, THE LESS THIRSTY THE WORLD BECAME

The Church gradually lost its understanding of salvation by grace and personal relationship with the Savior, but it managed to maintain some of the positive aspects of service to mankind. It was easier to feed the poor than to explain why the events of the Book of Acts ceased to be a normal part of the Christian life. As the Church lost its intimate relationship with the living God, it also lost its "saltiness" and usefulness in the world. The more the Church lost its salt, the less thirsty the world became.

The "mystics," the fervent "Marys" and God Chasers of previous centuries, braved excommunication, torture, and even death by burning to passionately seek His face. We are still being inspired by many of their powerful writings, penned in the heat of persecution and the intimacy of sweet communion with God.

Throughout history, God has always preserved a "remnant few" who pursued Him and lived according to His Word to the best of their ability. At times, He even ignited great revivals and restoration movements that revitalized whole nations and restored the light of His presence to entire generations. He is doing it again in our own generation!

We know this much: Martha needs Mary to remind her of the Lord's warning about choosing the "best portion." Mary, on the other hand, needs Martha to remind her to make her faith and intimacy with Divinity a real and loving comfort to the hurting humanity around her. Without Martha's input, Mary may be tempted to "hole up" in a cave of asceticism separated from society with no ability to help. One of the keys for any church to prosper in God's purposes is to allow its Marys to be Marys, and its Marthas to be Marthas.

ZEALOUSLY SERVING MARTHAS CAN EASILY STEP ON QUIETLY WORSHIPING MARYS

The biggest problem we face in this area today is teaching Martha how to appreciate and validate Mary's ministry, and vice versa. Marthas, by nature, tend to be more "take charge" and more aggressive in social situations and relationships. Zealously serving Marthas can easily step on quietly worshiping Marys. If there is no proper guidance or mediation between the two, Mary may well be overcome and swallowed up in Martha's enthusiastic pursuit (and delegation) of zealous service to humanity. One writer said of Martha:

> Martha is charge-taking throughout; this element, for good or for ill, pervades her whole character, and is part of her innermost being. She takes charge with heart, with hands, with lips;

she takes charge of her own house, of her brother's grave, of her sister, and of her Lord himself. She is busy with her hands preparing the supper for Jesus...Hands so active as hers would leave little for her sister to do, and nothing that could be done so well, yet Mary is a charge to her.[7]

It seems to me that Martha had learned to appreciate the power of Mary's service to the divinity of Jesus. Perhaps this explains Martha's "arrangement" after Lazarus' death, where she sent a message to Mary that Jesus had "called her." Is it possible that she sent for Mary hoping that her humble approach to the Lord through worship, adoration, and tender relationship would move the Master closer to Bethany, at the point where her abrupt challenge mingled with statements of faith had failed?

MARTHA SAW SOMETHING IN JESUS THAT SHE WANTED IN HER HOUSE

My aim is to highlight Martha's growing appreciation of Mary's anointing, not to point the finger of blame at Mary's "action-oriented" older sister. In her own way, Martha was a passionate God Chaser too. No one goes to the trouble Martha did just to offer a "home away from home" to a traveling preacher. She must have thought at first that Jesus was some itinerant rabbi who traveled with a large group of ever-hungry fishermen, tax collectors, and other assorted followers. *It didn't take her long to see something in Jesus that she wanted in her house at any cost,* even if she didn't fully understand the dual track of hospitality He required.

Mary must have appreciated her sister's abilities as well (although I'm sure they irritated her at times). Have you ever wondered how Mary acquired "a year's worth of wages" to buy the alabaster box of precious ointment she used to anoint Jesus? She wasn't married, and she had no trade that we know of. Since Mary lived in her older sister's house with her sometimes sickly brother, Martha was the most logical source for the money,[8] no matter how you reconstruct Mary's past.

John makes it clear that Mary anointed Jesus with costly anointing oil and wiped it away with her hair at least *twice*—once before her brother Lazarus fell sick and again in Bethany at the house of Simon the leper, just before Jesus' death and resurrection.[9]

In our first glimpse at Mary and Martha, the tension between the two reaches the point where open conflict begins to take place. This happens because two "sister anointings" often don't validate the value of one another's perspective.

In the second appearance, the sisters are united in grief over the loss of Lazarus, yet they still express their grief and seek relief in radically different ways. Martha's tendency to "take hold" and "make something happen" is still obvious in her manipulation of Mary through a messenger.

GOD IS BLESSED WHEN BOTH ANOINTINGS BLOOM IN HIS PRESENCE

In their third and final appearance in the Gospels, Mary and Martha demonstrate what can happen when they work together to serve the Lord. God is blessed when both anointings are allowed to bloom in His presence:

> *Then, six days before the Passover, Jesus came to Bethany, where Lazarus was who had been dead, whom He had raised from the dead. There they made Him a supper; and **Martha served**, but **Lazarus** was one of those who **sat at the table** with Him. Then **Mary took a pound of very costly oil of spikenard, anointed the feet of Jesus, and wiped His feet with her hair**. And the house was filled with the fragrance of the oil.[10]*

This time, Martha still serves, but her service of love is offered with no hint of the irritation or jealousy from the first occasion.[11] It almost seems that Mary approaches the Lord to anoint Him with Martha's blessing and support. In this sense, the fragrance that filled the room was produced by the loving unity of purpose apparent in the hearts of all three members of Martha's household.

Martha ministered to the Master's humanity, Lazarus ministered to the Lord's soul (after all, he had recent, personal knowledge of the path Jesus Himself would take), and Mary served both His divinity and humanity. (It was Mary who anointed the physical body of the Lamb of God just before it was offered on the altar of obedience at Calvary.) Martha served His humanity, Mary worshiped His divinity.

GOD DESCRIBES THE SERVICE OF MARY AND MARTHA SO WE CAN LEARN FROM THEM

This intimate dinner of honor was not recorded in the Scriptures simply because of its beauty or because it is a nice sequel to a tale. No, as with all Scripture, it was "...given by inspiration of God, and is profitable for doctrine, for reproof, for correction, for instruction in righteousness."[12] In other words, God describes the service of Mary and Martha in Simon's house because we are to *learn* from it.

No worship *service* will be complete apart from the free participation of Martha *and* Mary in the fullness of their gifts and abilities. The words of Jesus ring true today whether they apply to hurting people in an inner-city alleyway or to hurting people treading the carpeted aisles of suburban churches:

> ..."*Come, you blessed of My Father, inherit the kingdom prepared for you from the foundation of the world: for I was hungry and you gave Me food; I was thirsty and you gave Me drink; I was a stranger and you took Me in; I was naked and you clothed Me; I was sick and you visited Me; I was in prison and you came to Me.*"[13]

Mary cannot afford to keep Martha at arm's length; nor can Martha afford to push Mary out of her kitchen (lest she forget the importance of the "best portion"), or force her into the kitchen (and rob the Lord of her worship). When Mary remains joined to Martha, she won't have to worry about taking her faith to the streets or ministering to human needs. Martha will be there to remind her how to be blessed of the Father by blessing others. No one goes home hungry or naked where Martha is released to serve in her great anointing.

Martha, for her part, won't have to worry about losing the most important things in life through obsessive service with her hands only—Mary will sound the alarm when the Master enters the house. "It's time, Martha, quickly, take off the apron and follow me. The Master really is calling you...it's time to do the most important thing. The Father is here—He is waiting for your kiss."

Endnotes

1. See Matthew 5:25.

2. Tommy Tenney, *God's Dream Team: A Call to Unity* (Ventura, CA: Regal Books, a division of Gospel Light, 1999), Chapter 3, "Unity, Not Conformity," pp. 57-58.

3. Luke 10:38-39.

4. These events are described in Second Kings 4. According to James Strong, the root word for *Shunem* means "rest," and the Hebrew word for "persuaded" ("constrained" in the King James Version) means "latched on." See *Strong's Exhaustive Concordance of the Bible* (Peabody, MA: Hendrickson Publishers, n.d.), Hebrew definitions #7766, 7764, and 2388, respectively.

5. My point is that both women, the Shunammite woman and Martha, practiced "preemptive preparation" that ultimately released the resurrection power of God to raise the dead in their families. I do not mean to imply, in any way, that Elisha the prophet was the equal of Jesus Christ, the only begotten Son of God. However, it is proper to refer to both as "servants of God" (cf. Matthew 12:18, where Jesus is called "My Servant whom I have chosen").

6. A. Moody Stuart, *The Three Marys* (Carlisle, PA: The Banner of Truth Trust, 1984), p. 181. The author cites this quote from *La Famille de Bethanie*, by L. Bonnet, Pasteur de l'Église Française Protestante de Londres; also in an English translation.

7. Ibid.

8. A. Moody Stuart said of Martha's household in *The Three Marys*, "Their circumstances were such as at once to enable them to exercise hospitality, and to have given them plausible excuse for its omission had they sought it.

The family must no doubt have enjoyed the outward comfort which usually accompanies a wide influence; for they were well known and highly respected, not only in their native village but in Jerusalem, whence any of the Jews came to comfort the sisters on their brother's death. But, on the other hand, their means were not such as to surround them with servants, and to relieve them of the burdens of the household" (p. 151).

9. See John 11:1-2, where John writes, "It was that Mary who anointed the Lord with fragrant oil and wiped His feet with her hair, whose brother Lazarus was sick." Then go to the next chapter where John describes Mary's *second* and final anointing of Jesus in the house of Simon (see John 12:1-8, as well as similar accounts in Matthew 26:3-16 and Mark 14:1-10). What scholars do not know is whether or not Mary was the woman "who was a sinner" who anointed Jesus earlier in the house of a Pharisee named Simon (see Lk. 7:36-50). This is the only other mention of a woman breaking an alabaster box to anoint Jesus with oil and wipe His feet with her hair. However, even if Mary functioned as a sinner or prostitute earlier in her life and used the proceeds to purchase the first alabaster box of anointing fragrant oil, we know she was no longer the same once she met Jesus. That still points to Martha as Mary's primary source of financial support in subsequent purchases of anointing oil or ointment. Lazarus may have helped, but Martha seems to be the owner of the house.

10. John 12:1-3, emphasis mine.

11. A. Moody Stuart wrote of Martha's service in Simon the leper's house, "In the great feast after the resurrection of Lazarus, it is still written that 'Martha served.' Her work is necessary. Without the service there can be no feast at all, and none of the glorious incidents of the feast; and it is an honour to Martha, or to any daughter of Israel, to be called and made willing to minister to the earthly wants of Christ or his disciples. Yet it is Martha's first choice remaining to her, but purified and exalted; it is service still, but without care and distraction; it is service, but with no more murmuring at Mary for leaving her the second time to sit at the feet of Jesus; it is service, but in liberty and not in bondage..." (*The Three Marys*, pp. 184-185).

12. 2 Timothy 3:16.

13. Matthew 25:34-36.

Chapter Five

TOO HEAVY TO FLY

What Does It Mean to Be "Cumbered About"?

Just the other day as I attempted to check in for a flight, the airline gate agent sternly announced, "You have too many bags to fly, sir." I protested that I often flew with this many bags. He replied, "Not on this small plane!" I was forced to choose between not going at all or "lightening my load."

How often do we neglect Mary's ministry to pursue Martha's business during a typical day? Too many of us spend our lives choosing and consuming the "second-best things" of life instead of pursuing the "best thing" as Mary did.[1] Notice that I didn't say we choose "bad things." We tend to fill our lives with things that are "good" by most standards—they just aren't the best things.

My family helped me discover one of my "second-best" choices during a recent holiday season. The Tenney family is accustomed to its very hectic lifestyle. Everyone knows that when I'm home, I may be expected to attend at least a half-dozen crucial meetings each day and conduct phone conversations with people from around the United States and in other countries. (If I didn't "multi-task," I wouldn't "task" at all.) At this writing, I've been logging about 3,000 minutes per month on my cell phone!

During a particularly high-stress period just before the holiday season, I was rushing through my days and nights so I could take some time off with my family for a few days. The extra crunch just seemed to make things even worse.

I managed to totally frustrate my family. It was so bad that if they could have "kicked me out" temporarily, they would have. Finally, my wife and daughters picked up the phone and called my pastor on me! They contacted an elder statesman of the Body of Christ, and actually the pastor that I hold myself accountable to in New Orleans, and basically said, "We want you to do something about our dad. He's driving us nuts!"

He came to see me and "pastored" me with such kindness that I didn't even know he had slapped my wrist until he had already gone home. I especially remember one thing he told me, "Do you know what your kids told me is bothering them the most? It isn't your ministry—they are fine with everything you're doing."

I felt better at that point, but I wasn't ready for what he said next. My pastor said, "Your family said that when you're with them, you will interrupt those private family times to take a phone call from almost anybody. Yet, you tell the members of your family that their time is valuable." I knew what he said was true.

MY FAMILY PUT ME ON A "CELL PHONE DIET"

After my pastor left, I talked to my family and agreed to go on a "cell phone diet" over the holidays. I would like to tell you everything worked out smoothly, but my "cell phone diet" shared something in common with other kinds of diets. When my ministry director would call me, I'd sheepishly answer the cell phone and whisper, "Can't talk to you right now...I'll call you back later." When I thought no one in the family was looking, I'd sneak off downstairs and "cheat" on my diet by calling him back.

"Okay, what do you need? Hurry, quick!"

"What's wrong with you?"

"I'm on a cell phone diet..."

We do the same thing with God. We tell Him that we value His presence, but if somebody or something else "calls," we'll hop up from our position of worship to run off to the "kitchen" of human endeavor or the comfortable regimen of religious effort.

Somehow I think He just smiles (like my wife and kids smile at me, perhaps), and every once in a while He will tap us on the shoulder and say, "You're in sensory overload. Turn off your 'Martha cell phone' to the human realm every once in a while. Learn to just get away and spend some time with Me."

Sometimes you have to turn off one thing to turn on another. Perhaps you have heard one or more variations of the story of the "monkey and the coconut," in which a wild monkey is captured using a hollowed-out coconut shell. The shell is attached to a rope and filled with some attractive bait. The curious monkey puts its hand in the coconut to snatch the bait, but once the animal fills its hand with "loot," it is too large to pass through the small opening. The monkey is then easily captured with a net because it refuses to release its "good thing" inside the coconut to gain the "best thing"—its freedom.

We Make the Same Mistake Martha Made

When we lack the discipline and discernment to prioritize Divine presence over human performance, we are refusing to release our earthly "loot" to gain God's best. We make the same mistake Martha made and become what the King James Bible calls "cumbered."

> But Martha was **cumbered** about much serving, and came to Him, and said, Lord, dost Thou not care that my sister hath left me to serve alone? bid her therefore that she help me. And Jesus answered and said unto her, Martha, Martha, thou art careful and troubled about many things: but one thing is needful: and Mary hath chosen that good part, which shall not be taken away from her.[2]

Sometimes we can get into such sensory overload that we miss those moments of divine visitation or impartation. We get so busy that we forget to choose and pursue the best thing.

IS THAT YOUR EXCESS BAGGAGE?

The original Greek word translated as "cumbered" means "to drag all around."[3] Sometimes you're dragging around so much excess baggage, you can't feel it when He taps you on the shoulder. Both the New King James Version and the New International Version add another dimension when they say Martha was "distracted." The Scottish pastor and author, A. Moody Stuart, put it this way:

> Martha...may be taken as doing many things in the service of Jesus Christ, for the purpose of pleasing and honouring him. The case is a sadly common one; of doing much for Christ, yet caring less for Christ himself, his teaching, presence, and fellowship. Absent from Jesus she was working for Jesus, and she grudged to be left by her sister unaided in her work. She imagined that Christ had great need of her services, and that it would please him best to provide many things to honour him. But she mistook the character and calling of him who came not to be ministered unto but to minister, and to give his life a ransom for many. Jesus sought not hers, but her; he came not to receive but to give; he needed not Martha, but Martha was in urgent need of him.[4]

The Bible offers us a prescription and a cure for "encumbrance" in the Book of Hebrews:

> *Therefore we also, since we are surrounded by so great a cloud of witnesses, **let us lay aside** every weight, and the sin which so easily ensnares us, and let us run with endurance the race that is set before us."*[5]

RID YOURSELF OF ALL THAT WEIGHS YOU DOWN

My father and I examined the meaning of "lay aside" in this Scripture passage in a book we wrote entitled, *Secret Sources of Power*:

> According to an edition of the Bible containing comparative passages from up to 26 different translations, this passage in Hebrews 12:1 reads: *"stripping off every encumbrance"*

(Rotherham's translation), or "*Let us fling aside every encumbrance*," (Weymouth's translation). The Williams translation says it a little stronger: "*Let us throw off every impediment*." The 20th Century translation says, "*Let us lay aside everything that hinders us*," while the Knox translation reads, "*Let us rid ourselves of all that weighs us down*."[6]

Perhaps I should have called my enlightening experience over the holidays a "cell phone fast" instead of a "cell phone diet." It involved turning "off" the cell phone (and the chance to have a conversation using a fist full of electronics) so I could enjoy more satisfying (and vital) face-to-face conversations with my loving family.

Sometimes it takes a fast to clear the spiritual atmosphere and remove competing interferences. Remember that fasting doesn't do anything for God; it's for you. Picture yourself driving down the road with a good friend who is trying to have a meaningful conversation with you. The problem is that you have the radio up so loud, you have a hard time hearing what your friend is saying. Since it is your car, your friend is waiting for *you* to turn off the radio.

Fasting is when you reach over and turn off the radio so you can hear what your friend's saying. Fasting is when a busy father and husband turns off his cell phone to spend private time with his children and wife. In the spirit realm, sometimes we have to exercise discipline to bring balance to our lives by fasting—by turning off good things (all of our "Martha ministry") long enough to receive the *best* thing from the Friend who is closer than a brother.[7]

COMPASSION IS THE SEED OF THE MIRACULOUS

The cultural clutter and spiritual smog that permeates our lives just twists in my spirit because I'm convinced it is a primary culprit in our lack of compassion as Christians and disciples of Christ. Any serious examination of the New Testament Scriptures reveals that *compassion* is the seed or genesis of most of the miracles Jesus performed.

There are five Greek verbs translated as "compassion" in the New Testament, and all but one of them means to have pity, sympathy, or mercy on others. One of them, *splagchnizomai*, stands out as the main verb used most to describe how Jesus *felt* when He witnessed the suffering or pain of others.[8] *You may not be able to pronounce it, but you probably know what it feels like.*

The word *compassion* is really an understatement when compared to the true meaning of this unique Greek word. It literally means "to have the bowels yearn,"[9] and "to be moved as to one's inwards, to be moved with compassion."[10] Have you ever observed a sight that is so moving that it hurt you? If so, then you know the true meaning of the "Jesus-kind-of-compassion."

If compassion helped to fuel the miracles of Jesus, then we should seek and preserve the same kind of compassion in our own lives. That is why I'm careful about what I listen to and watch (and not just in terms of morality). I try to stay on a "diet" that keeps me from becoming overloaded with the wrong things. I have no wish to sound arrogant, but I try to guard my spiritual sensitivity.

When I was in college, I helped to build houses to earn extra money. I had calluses on certain parts of my hands from swinging the hammer because the two came into constant contact day after day.

SPIRITUAL AND EMOTIONAL "CALLUSES" DEVELOP WHERE YOU ARE EXPOSED

The same "callusing effect" takes place in your conscience when it comes into constant contact with extreme emotions, violence, or sensuality. Spiritual and emotional "calluses" develop at whatever point you are exposed to these extreme sensory barrages. God did not design the human body, soul, or spirit to take such sensory overload.

I have talked to people who worked in Somalia or Ethiopia where relief workers deal with thousands of children at the point of death and where entire populations of young and old are devastated by advanced stages of disease and starvation.

When I asked how they coped with such unending sorrow and pain, they said, "It always bothers you, but if you're there a while, you get a certain mind-set." One man told me, "If you didn't develop a little bit of callousness to protect you psychologically, you would go insane."

He explained that you have to disassociate yourself from the unrelenting pain of hurting humanity swirling around you. You have to get one step away and realize, "I'm just doing the best I can."

We can still feel the pain buried somewhere under layers of insulation, just as I can still "feel" the pressure of that hammer I used to swing all day long many years ago as a college student. However, if I were to pick up that same hammer today and use it for just one hour, it would put blisters on my hand.

Constant exposure and contact—whether to the holy or to the unholy—produces callousness in the human heart. Even sacred things can become common! Ask Uzzah! The mother of an infant can grow "deaf" to the less urgent cries of her child (even though everyone else around her may be pulling their hair out). In the same way, someone who works in an environment of constant profanity and ungodliness becomes nearly oblivious to their destructive effects on the human spirit.

"Marthas" in the Body of Christ tend to grow callous toward or overly familiar with the manifest presence of Divinity when they focus exclusively on the needs of humanity day after day.

"DAD, YOU CAN'T SEE THAT ONE"

I've learned to be careful about what I watch and hear each day. From time to time, my wife and daughters may want to see a sad movie, but they already know about Dad. One of my daughters will say, "Dad, you can't see that one," because they all know that if I see something that is very emotional or moving, then it will "put me over the edge" for two or three days. I'll just walk around for days thinking, *Oh my, I can't believe they died! Something should have been done.*

My family won't waste their time or money on bad films or immoral entertainment, but I have to avoid even good films with extremely emotional content. Why? I am determined to guard my spiritual sensitivity so that when the gentle breeze of the Holy Spirit, the heavenly Dove, blows through the Church or across my heart, then I will be sensitive to Him. I would rather deprive myself of exposure to "good things" so I can be sensitive to Him and receive God's best thing.

Occasionally I'll see one of the infomercials about the starving children in Somalia or Ethiopia, and I'll spend the next three days in intercessory prayer. (I generally avoid those programs, but sometimes the Holy Spirit works through those programs to help us release our ironclad grip on our hearts and checkbooks.) The key is the gentle leading of the Holy Spirit.

The media glut and sensationalism of modern life can easily and quickly desensitize us to the gentle voice and leading of the Lord. For this reason, we must learn how to prioritize our passions and remain sensitive to God's desires. I think Jesus was that way. In many places, the Gospel records tell us He was "moved with compassion." At other times He seemingly separated Himself from hurting humanity.

"I HAVE TO DO SOMETHING ABOUT IT"

Compassion played a crucial role in the miracles Jesus performed during His ministry. It seems to me that many of the greatest miracles occurred serendipitously; they just seemed to "happen" in the course of everyday events. Jesus would see a problem and basically say, "I have to do something about it."

In fact, I'm convinced that most of the time, Jesus did not "preplan" the miraculous; He happened upon it.[11] (I don't have a problem with pre-planned healing services; they can be effective tools to win the lost. Announce them and do whatever you can, but trust God to create the moment of miraculous intervention all on His own.)

The widow of Nain had no idea the Jewish rabbi named Jesus would intercept the funeral procession for her son. The Bible doesn't indicate that Jesus foresaw it either. He was just walking down the road leading through the city gate to reach His next appointment when the funeral procession passed through.

*And when He came near the gate of the city, behold, a dead man was being carried out, the only son of his mother; and she was a widow. And a large crowd from the city was with her. When **the Lord saw her, He had compassion on her** and said to her, "Do not weep." Then He came and touched the open coffin, and those who carried him stood still. And He said, "Young man, I say to you, arise." So he who was dead sat up and began to speak. And He presented him to his mother.*[12]

As a Jewish teacher, Jesus was very aware of the warnings in the Mosaic Law against touching a dead body. Any practicing Jew who touched a dead body was considered ceremonially unclean for seven days, even if he followed the guidelines for ceremonial cleansing. If he failed to go through the cleansing process, he was subject to the death penalty.[13]

Jesus avoided this problem in a simple but supernatural way: He never touched a dead body because, by the time His finger of divinity touched the lifeless shell of humanity, the body wasn't dead any longer!

The Bible says Jesus had a large crowd of people around Him when the "Jesus parade" was halted by death's convoy. Can you see all of the Lord' disciples and religious fans pressing toward Him in alarm when they saw Him boldly stop death's parade and approach the dead boy's coffin? "Don't touch him, Master! Don't touch it— You'll be unclean!" They knew that if He touched the body, then they couldn't hang around Him. They would have to twiddle their thumbs and handle things on their own for seven days. They still didn't understand that *the touch of God can kill living things like fruitless figs and restore life to dead things.*

HIS COMPASSION PUSHED HIM OVER THE EDGE OF INACTION

What would move Jesus so powerfully that He would challenge death, the most powerful natural law of human existence in the fallen realm? We know that He saw the widow lady's tears and felt deep grief. Evidently, when He saw that the woman had lost both her husband and her only son to death, He was so moved that His compassion pushed Him over the edge of inaction.

I think many North Americans and Europeans are so overexposed to emotional stimuli through the media that our capacity for compassion is greatly compromised or at least diminished. We see too much. Even the American Psychiatric Association has taken a strong position against media violence.

> "An oft quoted statistic still bears repeating: the typical American child watches 28 hours of television a week, and by the age of 18 will have seen 16,000 simulated murders and 200,000 acts of violence. As the evidence linking increased aggression to excessive exposure to violent entertainment has grown, psychiatrists, pediatricians, and other physicians and mental healthcare providers have joined the call for limits on the amount of violent depictions to which children are exposed.

> "...Children and adolescents are exposed to more media depictions of violence than ever before. Such depictions pervade not only television, but film, music, online media, videogames, and printed material. Commercial television for children is 50-60 times more violent than prime-time programs for adults, as some cartoons average more than 80 violent acts per hour...Again, these depictions desensitize children to the effects of violence, increase aggression, and help foster a climate of fear."[14]

The phrase, "video arcade effect," describes the way children can shoot people with a gun in cold blood and feel no emotion about their crime. Why? Many believe it is because some children practice killing people so much on video games that they no longer separate the reality of murder from the make-believe act on a video screen. To them, life itself is nothing but a game.

HAVING YOUR CONSCIENCE SEARED WITH A HOT IRON

Christians shouldn't be a bit surprised—God warned us about this in His Word long ago. The apostle Paul called it "having [your] conscience seared with a hot iron."[15] Sin wants to callus over your inner sensitivity to God's voice and dull the pain of sin so it no longer bothers you to do things you would never do under better circumstances.

Now for the good news: If you can raise your sensitivity level toward God's voice and toward sin, then you can raise the miraculous in your life. How can I claim such a thing? Remember that it was *compassion* that moved Jesus into the realm of the miraculous.

"Let's get out of the service— they want time among themselves again."

I seem to remember the late John Wimber saying, "You can't tell the good news and be the bad news." This happens when you try to mix compassion with apathy, wrong priorities, or sin. This is one of the most costly consequences to being "cumbered." Consider this description of Martha and ask whether you have become "good news" or "bad news" to the people you meet or work with each day:

> Martha chooses many things, many cares, many burdens, and would not be happy without them. She is not happy with them, for they cannot give her peace, but neither can she rest without them … Her burden is of choice, and not of necessity. Jesus did not thank Martha for her many things, far less for her many troubles about them; and all that was required might well have been wrought by her active hands with an unburdened spirit. But her heart loves the care, the cumbrance, and the manifold distractions. These were once the portion of her soul, and to them she is still too fondly wedded.[16]

Have you ever sensed the frustration of the Holy Spirit caused by human callousness? It seems to happen often in the middle of church services, when there's a river of worship flowing upward and the presence of God is rich. Then someone feels it's time to move on, so they say, "Let's get on with the service."

This often grieves the Spirit and causes God to say, "Let's get out of the service—they want time among themselves again." We shouldn't be surprised when the manifest presence of God vanishes instantly. This is a case where "people pressure crowds out Presence."

There are times when it is "right" or appropriate to move from worship to something else. (This is usually when we genuinely sense that God is ready to bless His people through His Word or through ministry to personal needs.) I'm not trying to judge anyone who cuts short a worship service; my point is that we must honor the Holy Spirit. Paul made it clear that we can grieve the Holy Spirit through our words and deeds.[17]

I pray that God will give us the sensitivity to know when to wear which hat: Martha's hat of service to humanity or Mary's hat of worship before Divinity. We desperately need God's wisdom day by day. Meanwhile, we willingly live in the tension between the two ministries of the Church.

When the infamous "cliff-hanger" U.S. Presidential election was dragging on week after week, one day my youngest daughter came in to ask me some questions. Like millions of other adult American voters at the time, I was trying my best to get a clue about what was really going on. So I said, "S-h-h-h, I'm trying to hear what's happened."

In her most disgusted tone, my daughter summed up the attitude of the whole nation at that time when she said, "I'll be so glad when *somebody* is president!"

What she was really saying was, "I want you to pay attention to me." I was concerned about many things, but in my daughter's eyes, only one thing was needed. Right then she needed her daddy, and that outweighed my temporary need to know who won some election.

DROP THE MANY CUMBERING CONCERNS OF MARTHA

Martha probably loved Jesus just as much as Mary did, but unlike Mary, the elder sister was *cumbered* by many concerns. We need to learn how and when to drop the many cumbering concerns of Martha so we can minister to Divinity through the worship of Mary. In the words of A. Moody Stuart:

> Martha represents the legal inquirer, Mary the believer in Jesus Christ. But Martha represents also the legal Christian, working many things that give Christ little honour or pleasure, peradventure none; and Mary sets forth the believing soul alive to its own wants, and *honouring Christ by ever hungering for him, and by receiving him as the very bread of its life.*[18]

Endnotes

1. See Luke 10:42.

2. Luke 10:40-42 KJV.

3. James Strong, *Strong's Exhaustive Concordance of the Bible* (Peabody, MA: Hendrickson Publishers, n.d.), Greek definition #4049.

4. A. Moody Stuart, *The Three Marys* (Carlisle, PA: The Banner of Truth Trust, 1984), p. 169.

5. Hebrews 12:1, emphasis mine.

6. T.F. Tenney and Tommy Tenney, *Secret Sources of Power: Rediscovering Biblical Power Points* (Shippensburg, PA: Fresh Bread, an imprint of Destiny Image Publishers, 2000), Chapter 1: "Unload the Weight of Life and the Pressing Demands of Other People," p. 6, with the following citation on page 13: "All the translations noted are cited in *26 Translations of the NEW TESTAMENT*, Curtis Vaughan, gen. ed. (Oklahoma City, Oklahoma: Mathis Publishers—Copyright 1967 by Zondervan Publishing House, Grand Rapids, Michigan), p. 1107."

7. See Proverbs 18:24.

8. This word is transliterated as *splagchnizomai*. This conclusion and support for it was drawn in part from the work of W.E. Vine (Old Testament edited by F.F. Bruce), *VINE'S Expository Dictionary of Old and New Testament Words* (Old Tappan, NJ: Fleming H. Revell Company, 1981), pp. 218-219.

9. *Strong's*, Greek definitions #4697, 4698.

10. *VINE'S*, word definition "A.2." for "compassion, compassionate," on the Greek verb transliterated as *splanchnizomai*, p. 218.

11. One possible exception may be the resurrection of Lazarus. In this situation, it appears that by the time Martha's message reached Jesus, He couldn't have reached Lazarus before his death due to travel distances. However, it is clear that He *knew* in advance that Lazarus needed a resurrection, not a healing.

12. Luke 7:12-15.

13. See Numbers 19:11-13.

14. American Psychiatric Association, Public Information section of the official APA web site, from the article titled, "Psychiatric Effects of Media Violence," www.psych.org/public_info/media_violence.cfm. Accessed 4/9/01.

15. See 1 Timothy 4:1-2 KJV.

16. Stuart, *The Three Marys*, p. 171.

17. See Ephesians 4:30.

18. Stuart, *The Three Marys*, p. 170, emphasis mine.

Chapter Six

Bi-Polar Spirituality

Am I Mary or Am I Martha?

An unending conflict surges quietly in your heart this very moment, and in one sense, it is God's doing. We are all constantly torn between the two siblings of the human soul represented by Mary and Martha. You live in a constant tension between two "poles" of human experience because Mary and Martha live inside you. You don't know whether to feed the poor or take time to pray.

You might as well admit the truth and ask, "Am I Mary or am I Martha?" You can't help yourself apart from divine intervention because, at best, you are a divided house, a "bi-polar personality" gripped in a seemingly unending clash of Mary and Martha's differing worldviews and ideas.

What did Jesus say about divided houses? "Every kingdom divided against itself is brought to desolation, and every city or house divided against itself will not stand."[1] But have you noticed that God isn't very disturbed by houses that suffer *temporary* bouts of strife and division? He just doesn't want them to stay that way.

Jesus launched His conquest of satan's kingdom with a ragtag group of disciples who were always arguing about who was the best, the brightest, and the most beloved in God's eyes. He chose to build His Church using *individual* believers from every tribe and nation because we can come together only through the supernatural power of the cross.

He created you and me with a "Mary and Martha" inside. Now it is up to us to yield to His hand so Mary and Martha can come together in us to make humanity's house a habitation for Divinity.

I believe we are learning, as Mary and Martha did, that our house isn't complete when one or the other is missing. Martha needs Mary, and believe it not, Mary needs Martha.

Without Martha's practical Christian service and work ethic operating in your personality, you will find it hard to maintain a godly witness among other people. For some reason, people expect Christians to act selflessly to help others. Many in the Church would rather gather at the river of God for fellowship and gospel singing than gather under the bridge of homelessness to dispense equal servings of food, clothing, and unconditional love to society's "unlovable untouchables."

At the same time, the Martha in us must understand that without Mary's single-minded devotion to Jesus, all the service we perform for the people "under the bridge" will amount to little less than a soon-forgotten "Band-aid" on eternally wounded hearts. Our good works and deeds of kindness will open human hearts, but they cannot save them. We can warm human hearts through acts of charity, but only Jesus can cleanse them from sin and give them eternal life in God's presence.

WORK LIKE MARTHA, WORSHIP LIKE MARY

God wants us to honor Him *and* bless men in Christ's name. The only way to do both is to work like Martha and worship like Mary. The real problem is how to make them work and worship *together*.

Did you know that even Jesus Christ and Paul the apostle experienced this struggle between the "Mary and Martha" of the heart?

Consider Jesus, wrestling back and forth between "Martha's will to live" and "Mary's will to die" in the garden of Gethsemane. Not once but twice He wrestled with the Mary and Martha viewpoints in agonized prayer.

First, He prayed,

O My Father, if it is possible, let this cup pass from Me; neverthe-less, not as I will, but as You will."[2]

The second time, the world's only sinless human petitioner prayed,

"O My Father, if this cup cannot pass away from Me unless I drink it, Your will be done."[3]

Paul the apostle wasn't perfect, but God chose him to write a large portion of the New Testament passages. This great church leader and God Chaser described his fierce inner struggle this way:

For I am hard-pressed between the two, having a desire to depart and be with Christ, which is far better. Nevertheless to remain in the flesh is more needful for you. And being confident of this, I know that I shall remain and continue with you all for your progress and joy of faith.[4]

If we recast Paul's statements in "Mary and Martha terms," they might sound like this: "The Mary in me would rather go on to be with Christ, which is far better. Nevertheless, God spoke through the Martha in me and assured me that I am more needed here in the earthly realm to help your progress and joy of faith."

God wanted the "Martha" in Paul to help him take the message of "Mary" in his heart to the struggling young church about to face a new wave of persecution and difficulty.

YOU MUST BE "SPIRITUALLY SIGHTED" TO LEAD THE SPIRITUALLY BLIND

It is difficult for you to take someone else "higher" to God's realm when you barely know His address yourself. You must be spiritually "sighted" like Mary to lead the spiritually blind into the light of His presence.

Martha's mistake was to accuse Jesus of "not caring" that Mary had abandoned the kitchen to worship at His feet.[5] Her virtue was that she seemed to learn from her mistake. Evidently, Martha began to appreciate Mary's sensitivity to Jesus and the pathway it created to His heart. Perhaps that is why she "arranged" for Mary to think that Jesus had called her after Lazarus died.[6]

I wonder if Martha hoped that Mary's worshipful tears could accomplish what her confident confrontation could not—to bring the miracle-working Jesus into their painful crisis. Practical Martha probably took extra care to heed Mary's insights after the first disaster in Bethany. She would never again miss a divine appointment with the Master.

The Martha in you needs to tap the power of Mary's spiritual sensitivity, just as Bartimaeus "borrowed" the eyes and perceptions of others to compensate for his natural blindness. As I noted in *The God Catchers*:

> Many times, in the moment of our hunger, we don't know which way to cry out, what to say, what to pray, or what to sing! Blind Bartimaeus didn't see Jesus until *after* he had received a miracle. He had to take somebody's word for it that the cause of the disturbance was Jesus and that He was close.
>
> There may be times in your life when your spiritual "senses" seem deafened or blinded, and you won't be able to sense the nearness of God. In times of spiritual sensory deprivation, you must walk by faith and stand on His Word. You may have to take someone else's word that He is in the house. Whether it is a worship leader, a spouse, or a preacher, pay close attention when the person says, "He's close."
>
> In that moment, reach out for Him with all the passion and hunger in your heart—"feel after Him, and find Him, though He be not far from every one of us."[7,8]

In the biblical story, blind Bartimaeus sought the help of "sighted" parade watchers to initiate a divine encounter with Jesus and receive his sight. The soulish and sometimes "spiritually challenged" Martha within us needs the vision and perception of the spiritually "sighted" Mary in our hearts. Unified pursuit of Divinity is perhaps the only way to end the inward struggle within us.

Sometimes your soul needs to grow quiet and listen to the gentle whispers of the spirit. The worshipful song of the heart can help you find your way through the labyrinth of cold reason and the heat of unchecked emotions.

A. Moody Stuart's comparison of the biblical Mary and Martha also may cast light on the nature of the "sibling battle" that goes on within each one of us at times:

> Martha begins with troubled working; and being reproved, she ends with single-hearted yet homely service. Mary begins with quiet hearing, and ends with noble work, great and abiding forever. To work is easier than to hear, because working can well be desired for its own sake. Work is an end to itself. Though not one jot of real good be done; yet there is work; and the soul, occupied with it, rests in it. Though not one tittle of the work has been accepted by God, yet the worker has pleased himself, and finds a treacherous peace. But the fruit of hearing is less easily mistaken.[9]

GOD HAS CLEAR PREFERENCES ABOUT THE THINGS WE DO FOR HIM

God loves us all without partiality or what the King James Version calls "respect of persons."[10] Yet it is obvious that He has clear preferences about *the things we do for Him.*

According to the Book of Genesis, God preferred the blood sacrifice of Abel to the bloodless gifts from Cain's labor.[11] On the other hand, He clearly preferred the bloodless worship and adoration of passionate David to the bloody mass sacrifices offered by passionless priests in the name of religious tradition.[12]

In each case, the motives and passions of the giver's heart mattered more than the outward nature of the gifts they offered to God.[13] In our ongoing battle between the will and works of Martha and the passionate brokenness of Mary, God's preference is clear. He is not attracted to our strengths, but He is irresistibly drawn to our displayed weakness and "witheredness." Again Mr. Stuart said:

> Martha works at the beginning, and murmurs because her sister sits and works not. Sitting and hearing in that hour are but sloth and idleness to her; out of season with one sister, because Christ needs bodily service then; in season with the other, because it is the Lord's own precious time for ministering to the soul. *But it is Mary's turn now*, and she achieves a deed renowned through all the earth, and embalming her name through all ages; a work more grateful to the heart of Jesus than any that ever cheered him in his sorrows, from his birth in Bethlehem to his death on Calvary; a work of all others the most worthy of him, and the most exalting to his name; a work which he so prized that he sealed it with the announcement, altogether singular, that where the gospel shall be preached in the whole world, this also shall be told in memorial of Mary.[14]

HIS PRESENCE COMES TO BREAK BREAD AND RAISE THE DEAD

When passion returns to the Church, Presence comes down the aisle. When Mary's passion overtakes Martha's heart or overcomes the cynicism and criticism of the passionless, His Presence comes to break bread and raise the dead.

Mary is quick to say, "I'll sacrifice my dignity to have an encounter with Deity," but Martha must learn that when His manifest presence is in the house, she must say, "I'll sacrifice the best work my hands have done for humanity in exchange for one moment of service through worship in the presence of Deity."

Passion for Deity makes complacency stick out like the prover-bial "sore thumb"—it also highlights the second-best aspects of ser-vice to humanity when Deity is "manifested in the house." Mary's unquenchable passion often makes "Martha's-heart disciples" uncomfortable and even resentful. Passion makes everyone else uncomfortable until Jesus endorses it.

Martha's anointed service to humanity should really prepare, support, and enable Mary's anointed service to Deity (as in Martha's service at the final supper in Simon's house).

THE DIVINE BLUEPRINT FOR LIFE'S PRIORITIES

The question isn't whether or not you should heed the Martha in your heart and serve humanity's needs in the Church (and on the street), or follow Mary's lead and serve the desires of Deity. *You must do both.* The question has to do with the priorities and passions of the heart. Jesus gave us the divine blueprint for life's priorities when He said:

> ..."You shall love the Lord your God with all your heart, with all your soul, with all your strength, and with all your mind," and "your neighbor as yourself."[15]

Come on, Mary! Come on, Martha! Come on, Bartimaeus! Remind us that His presence in our hearts and lives is more impor-tant than everything else.

Have you noticed that crises and problems seem to bring out the Martha in most people? (Only a fortunate few seem to land on their knees like Mary in times of trouble.) If your "Martha side" takes the driver's seat in a given situation, you probably become "action-oriented." You feel driven to "do something" about the problem, and prayer and worship are often excluded from the action plan because, to Martha, they have the feel and look of "inaction."

Martha is a good ally in any situation where hard work and dili-gence in service to humanity can get the problem solved. These things can bring disaster, however, if the problem calls for the hand or mind of Divinity rather than humanity.

The "Martha" in you will instinctively throw your "strengths" at any problem or challenging situation, whether those strengths involve intelligence quotients, physical stamina, strength of will, analytical genius, persuasive skills, or any number of other native skills and abilities.

The problem is that God isn't attracted to your strengths. *He is drawn to your weakness.* The "rebuking Martha" who approaches the Lord in a presumptive or aggressive stance will herself be rebuked and told to assume Mary's position on her knees.

"The proven solution for the Martha in you is simple— extend your weakness to Him rather than your strength."

The proven solution for the Martha in you is simple—extend your *weakness* to Him rather than your strength. That's what the man with the withered right hand did the day Jesus came to the local church to preach.

> …[Jesus] *said to the man who had the withered hand, "Arise and stand here." And he arose and stood. Then Jesus said to them* [the scribes and Pharisees], *"I will ask you one thing: Is it lawful on the Sabbath to do good or to do evil, to save life or to destroy?" And when He had looked around at them all, He said to the man, "Stretch out your hand." And he did so, and his hand was restored as whole as the other.*[16]

When Jesus asked the man to stretch forth his hand, *He didn't tell him which hand to stretch out.* He had a withered hand, and he had a good hand. Jesus didn't tell him which hand to use; He just said, "Stretch out your hand." It was the man's decision to make: "Do I reveal my strength, or do I reveal my weakness and my witheredness to Him in front of all of these people?"

When we come to church or meet with our friends, we try to pretend like everything is okay (but it really isn't). In the end, we extend our "good hand" to disguise and hide our weakness from humanity—and we miss our moment with Divinity. It happens every time we appeal to Him out of our strength instead of our weakness.

Something in the eyes of Jesus told the physically challenged man, "It's okay to pull your witheredness from its hiding place in the pocket or folds of your garment." If that man had stretched forth his good hand, I think he would have gone home with a withered hand as he had hundreds of times before. Instead, he dared to stretch forth his withered hand and publicly reveal his weakness. Jesus sent him home with two good hands and the testimony of a lifetime. (What will *you* dare to extend toward Him?)

"We extend our 'good hand' to disguise and hide our weakness from humanity— and we miss our moment with Divinity."

When your "Martha side" seems to be overtaking your life and smothering the passion of your Mary heart, don't bother to put your strength on display. Move to a place of His presence and reveal your weakness and witheredness to Him. He will meet you at the very point where you decide to sacrifice your dignity—and your works— for a moment with Deity.

Restore Mary's heart of God-dependency to Martha's tendency of self-dependency. Just pull your brokenness and witheredness from the folds of your garment and say, "No, it's *not* okay. I desperately need Him! I am so desperate for an encounter with Him that I will expose my weakness in front of everyone if necessary. I must see Him."

This is your moment to expose your weakness and receive His strength. The *best* thing that could ever happen to you is for your "Martha" to join your "Mary" at the Master's feet.

The view of life seen from the feet of Deity differs greatly from the skewed worldview Martha sees from the table of her labors.

"The view of life seen from the feet of Deity differs greatly from the skewed worldview Martha sees from the table of her labors."

Sometimes we find godly balance between the Mary and Martha within us by changing our perspective or viewpoint of things. The first focuses on every expression and word of the Master; the second scans every expression and exasperation of mankind.

If you are torn between two conflicting ways to approach a problem, instruct your Mary to consider Martha's view and make sure Martha reexamines the situation from Mary's position at the Master's feet. *The place of peace is somewhere between the two.*

God is searching for the Mary in you, for the passionate worshiper who will worship Him in spirit and in truth. Yet He also considers it your *duty* to "offer up your body as a living sacrifice" to Him (a duty that the Martha in you would quickly answer with a passionate "Yes, Lord!").[17]

People whose lives are no longer their own don't balk at the idea of doing hard work in the name of Christ.[18] Dead men made alive in Christ have no ego obstructing their decision to serve at the bedside of dying AIDs patients or lovingly restraining those enduring the *delirium tremens* of chronic alcoholism or years of intravenous heroin addiction.

Spiritually dead people who have been given new life in Christ simply do all as a service unto Him, as a composition of worship orchestrated and played for God through their own lives.

Jesus Christ never asked us to throw out our bodies or discard Martha's practical service as worthless. He simply asks that we keep our priorities and passions straight. How? Just do what He says. Deny yourself daily, take up your cross, and follow Him—offer yourself as a vehicle to transport Divinity into the world of lost, hurting, and searching humanity.[19] It is there, where Divinity meets humanity in the place of hospitality, that you find your true self.

The point of balance between conflicting priorities saturates the Master's teachings: "But seek first the kingdom of God and His righteousness, and all these things shall be added to you."[20] (Seek Him and His face, and He will joyfully give you what is in His hand.) He also said:

> *Nevertheless I have this against you, that you have left your first love. Remember therefore from where you have fallen; repent and do the first works...*[21]

"Offer yourself as a vehicle to transport Divinity into the world of lost, hurting, and searching humanity."

Return to your *first* love and do the *first* works...discard your lesser lovers and love your First Love with all of your heart, soul, mind, and strength like Mary. And take a lesson from Martha—make every effort to "love your neighbor as you love yourself."

Mary and Martha, it is time to come together and create a place of hospitality where Divinity and humanity can meet.

Endnotes

1. Matthew 12:25.

2. Matthew 26:39b.

3. Matthew 26:42b.

4. Philippians 1:23-25.

5. See Luke 10:40.

6. See John 11:28. This passage seems to imply that Martha "expanded" the message from "the Master is here" to include what was never stated explicitly in the narrative—that He had "called" for Mary.

7. Luke 6:6-11.

8. Tommy Tenney, *The God Catchers* (Nashville, TN: Thomas Nelson Publishers, 2000), pp. 70-71.

9. A. Moody Stuart, *The Three Marys* (Carlisle, PA: The Banner of Truth Trust, 1984), pp. 187-188.

10. See Romans 2:11; Ephesians 6:9; 1 Peter 1:17.

11. See Genesis 4:3-7; Hebrews 11:4.

12. God said in the 50th Psalm, *"If I were hungry, I would not tell you; for the world is Mine, and all its fullness. Will I eat the flesh of bulls, or drink the blood of goats? Offer to God thanksgiving, and pay your vows to the Most High. Call upon Me in the day of trouble; I will deliver you, and you shall glorify Me"* (Ps. 50:12-15). In Psalm 51, David said, *"For You do not desire sacrifice, or else I would give it; You do not delight in burnt offering. The sacrifices of God are a broken spirit, a broken and a contrite heart—these, O God, You will not despise"* (Ps. 51:16-17).

13. By *passion*, I refer to what I call an "ardent affection or love for and devotion to God and His purposes." It is the heart and soul of a true God Chaser, as well as the stock and trade of the genuine God Catcher.

14. Stuart, *The Three Marys*, p. 196, emphasis mine.

15. Luke 10:27.

16. Luke 6:8-10.

17. See Romans 12:1.

18. See 1 Corinthians 6:20; Luke 14:26.

19. See Luke 9:23 and Romans 12:1 once again.

20. Matthew 6:33.

21. Revelation 2:4-5.

Chapter Seven

YOUR SHOES DON'T FIT ME!

Seasons Outside the Comfort Zone

In eight brief words, a good friend of mine described one of the most important keys to solving the conflict between Marys and Marthas in the modern Church. He spoke up after he and a number of other friends of the ministry had discussed the topic with me for some time. His words promptly launched us into a fresh round of excited personal insights.

"I think I figured it out," he said. "I am a Martha having a Mary experience." Does that make him a spiritual schizophrenic? I can walk in your shoes but that doesn't make them comfortable. Martha's shoes don't fit Mary. Neither will Mary's shoes fit Martha. God made you to fit "in your own skin."

Another friend involved in the discussion described an encounter he and his wife had that changed their lives forever. He is a respected physician in our region of Louisiana, and he described what occurred while he and his wife were visiting a large city.

Just as the couple walked out of the front door of a very nice restaurant, they came face to face with a homeless woman who was obviously in need. Somehow my friend sensed that this chance encounter was really a divine appointment despite the range of emotions and cautions that flooded his thoughts.

The couple decided to take a risk and offered to take the woman back into the restaurant and buy her a hot meal.[1] These friends are true God Chasers, and this man became a doctor because he cares about people. Yet every time he tells this story, a flood of tears punctuates his words.

With the decision made and the offer accepted, my friends accompanied the woman into the restaurant to make sure she received the food she needed and was treated properly. They soon noticed that she was piling a lot of extra food on her plate—more than most of us could eat in one sitting. The woman must have sensed their concern because she explained that the extra food was for the hungry children who were waiting for her.

TWO LOUISIANA MARYS HAVE AN UNFORGETTABLE MARTHA EXPERIENCE

My doctor friend and his wife are very compassionate people, but their lives were changed that night. They had a divine encounter—not with a hungry God but with a hungry woman—and it became a spiritual epiphany for them. They realized that they were Marys who had become so spiritually minded that God wanted to bring balance to their lives. He did it by leading those two "Louisiana Marys" into a Martha experience they would never forget.

Whether we like it or not, *God leads all of us into seasons on the other side* of our natural comfort zones. If we yield to His hand, even the discomfort of spiritual adjustment can bring a life-changing epiphany of His presence to our hearts.

It doesn't matter whether you are a Martha having a Mary experience or a Mary reluctantly having a Martha experience—God wants to build a comfort zone for Himself in your life and in the Church. That means He wants to have both Mary and Martha, both parts of the whole, at work in your life.

I've noticed that Marys seem to have the biggest problem with these seasons on the other side. A large percentage of "God Chasers" probably consider themselves to be Marys, and they may say to themselves, *Okay, I can see God pulling a Martha into the things of the spirit, but would He really pull a Mary into a natural area such as serving the poor?*

I think the defining line between the ministries of Mary and Martha is the difference between *passion* and *compassion*. In my mind, passion defines our vertical love for Him and compassion defines our horizontal love for mankind.

The cross of Christ pictures God's perfect plan for chasing God while serving man. The vertical beam of Calvary's tree bridges the gap between God in Heaven and fallen men on earth in perfect obedience and adoration for the Father. The Lord's outstretched arms on the horizontal crossbeam of personal sacrifice openly reveal the Son of Man's compassion and open invitation for fallen man.

WE NEED *BOTH* COMPONENTS OF CALVARY'S CROSS

Mary's vertical ministry goes straight to the heart of God and Martha's ministry goes straight from the heart of God to the heart of man. We need *both* components of Calvary's cross at work in our hearts and churches.

In practical terms, we shouldn't be surprised when we feel "pulled" in two different directions according to the seasons of our lives. God loves us too much to leave us in spiritual stagnation. He is constantly planning divine encounters with us to keep our relationship with Him fresh and alive. As I wrote in *The God Catchers*, I can almost hear the Lord tell His amazed angels, "No, nothing is more important to Me than preplanning encounters with My children."[2]

In one season, you may feel the gentle pull of the Spirit into the well of spiritual passion for God's presence. In the next, you may feel drawn to enter the waters of God's compassion for the people Jesus died for. Most of the time, the "pulling" you sense is the persistence of God's will flowing around the resistance of your will. In His great love He may cause you to "stumble" across Him unawares in your journey to the other side and reawaken fresh spiritual passion in your life.

If you are a Martha having a Mary experience, you may enter a season when all you want to do is just pray and worship. Don't feel guilty for your brief absence from the works of compassionate service you so enjoy—it is God's doing and it's okay.

Just enjoy a holy honeymoon with Him. Devote yourself to the totally abandoned pursuit of God. At the moment you least expect it you may hear God's still, small voice whisper, "Get ready. After you know what it means to have your hair catch on fire in the supercharged atmosphere of the upper room of worship, you will hear a gentle knock at the door."

God may send to you the Grecian widows of Stephen's day who need your table-waiting skills or to a little homeless lady in need of a hot meal in a modern city.

If you are a Mary, then you too must spend certain seasons on the other side of your personal preference. Be of good cheer; it is for your own good. God appreciates every good gift and offering of praise and worship that you give to Him, but He is determined to equip you and conform you to Jesus' balanced image.[3]

Seasons on the Other Side *Will* Stretch You

The investment of seasons on the other side is the only way you can stretch your heart and soul enough to fulfill God's divine purposes in both the vertical and horizontal dimensions of His love. It seems I read somewhere, "*By this we know love, because He laid down His life for us. And we also ought to lay down our lives for the brethren.*"[4] Sometimes you lay down your life with serving hands; sometimes you offer the sacrifice with bended knee and a flood of passionate intercessory tears. God expects you to be ready for both.

Consider Judas, the disciple who betrayed Jesus after spending three years within touching distance of the Son of God. What was so wrong with this man that he would exchange his personal relationship with loving Divinity for a handful of "treasure" from jealous humanity that ranks one step below Heaven's road paving material?

Perhaps the problem was that *Judas was a Martha who never had a true Mary experience.*

As treasurer for the 12, Judas led others to believe he knew how to manage earthly resources when he was really a thief.[5] Evidently he knew even less about investing the riches God truly treasures—the unconditional love of the human heart.

WHAT HAPPENS WHEN GOD'S PRESENCE OVERFLOWS IN *YOUR* LIFE?

Stephen started out in the Martha ministry as an anointed table waiter known for his faith in God. He moved into a Mary ministry when his relationship with Divinity became so strong that the presence of God began to overflow in his life in the form of miracle-working faith and power. Stephen was a Martha who had such a life-changing Mary experience that his fiery zeal helped make him history's first martyr for Christ.[6]

Peter the fisherman was a "Let 's get something done and let's do it *now*!" kind of man. When he put his best foot forward, it generally ended up in his mouth.

This impetuous fisherman believed in putting his sword where his heart was, and we see no biblical evidence that he was a great man of prayer or meditation in the years he traveled with Jesus. For instance, all the disciples slept while Jesus prayed alone in the garden of Gethsemane, but the Lord singled out Peter for rebuke (perhaps because he was the natural leader of the 12).[7]

When Judas led representatives of the high priest and a contingent of soldiers to the garden to arrest Jesus, it was Peter who pulled out his sword and cut off the right ear of Malchus, the servant of the high priest. Jesus stepped in to stop the violence and heal the man's ear. Then He warned Peter that those who live by the sword would die by the sword.[8] I wonder how God has to disarm the disciples before He can heal the wounded.

In the natural, Peter was bold, brash, and born for the battle. He was the leader, even when he was going in the wrong direction, but he seemed to have a lingering addiction to the approval of men that plagued him throughout most of his early ministry. He bragged that he would rather die with Jesus than deny Him, and the rest of the disciples joined him in the vow. Later Peter denied the Lord three times in embarrassment and fear when a housemaid accused him of being Jesus' friend.[9]

Things changed after he had a radical *Mary* experience in the Upper Room and was filled with the Holy Spirit. He stepped out of that prayer meeting and preached the world's first apostolic sermon with such boldness that three thousand people answered his altar call on Jerusalem's streets in broad daylight.[10]

MIRACLES HAPPENED EVERY TIME HE PRAYED

Every time the Bible mentions that Peter prayed, we notice miraculous things happened soon afterward. After Peter went to a rooftop to pray, he received the heavenly vision from God revealing that lowly Gentiles were included in His salvation plan.[11] On the other hand, things went badly when the apostle left his prayer closet to socialize with his highly placed Jewish Pharisee friends. It seems he conveniently forgot the heavenly vision so he could enjoy man's blessings and approval. It took Paul's public rebuke for racism and religious favoritism to put Peter back on course.[12]

Peter was an action-oriented leader more than a consistent "feeder of sheep" in the natural. When Jesus restored balance to his life after the resurrection, He specifically told Peter three times to feed and tend His sheep.[13] We know Peter successfully crossed over to the "other side" of his nature because he became a true feeder of sheep. Christians are still "feeding" on the spiritual wealth contained in Peter's characteristically brief apostolic letters to the saints.[14]

GOD IS INTERESTED IN THE FINAL SPRINT TO THE FINISH LINE

It is Peter's "humanness" that encourages us the most. I would love to know how many people have said to themselves in difficult times, *If Peter could do it, then I can do it too.* Peter's flaws must have inspired hundreds of thousands of sermons over the centuries, but God's mercy in his life has inspired millions of believers to get back up and try again. God didn't focus on Peter's rocky start or frequent falls as much as on his final sprint to the finish line.

The same man who denied Jesus when accused by a servant girl willingly laid down his life for Christ at the end of his ministry. According to church tradition, Peter asked his executioners to crucify him upside down because he wasn't worthy to die on the cross as His Savior did.

It was a series of Mary experiences "on the other side" that transformed Peter from an ear-slasher and betrayer into a man who would say, in essence, "I'm finished with the cutting and slashing of my early years. I know the One who loves me. Now I'll let you cut on *me* if you have to."

Expect to experience transition and movement from one season to the next in your life. *Don't act so offended when God's purposes require you to go back and forth between Martha's kitchen and Mary's position.*

It Takes Mary *and* Martha to Build the House

God takes you to Martha's kitchen when He has work to be done in the *earthly realm* with willing hands and a compassionate heart. He moves you into Mary's position when He needs something done in the *heavenly realm* with a passionate heart and hands raised in praise and adoration. It has been said, "It takes a village to raise a child." I'm thinking it takes a Mary *and* a Martha to build a house of comfort for our dual-natured Savior and the people He loves.

In a sense, it is all the same to Him whether you are a Mary having a Martha experience or a Martha having a Mary experience. Jesus set the standard, but Mary and Martha helped define it for us. You will do well as long as your *heart* stays in *the Mary position* and your *servant body* stays in *the Martha position*. This is a picture of the heart of a worshiper and the attitude of a servant joined in unity.

Real revival is not just when God shows up. Neither is real revival when crowds of mankind show up. Real revival is when God and man show up at the same time at the same place.

In order for that to happen you must have credibility in both realms: you need Mary's ability to call for God and see Him come, linked with Martha's credible reputation for caring for hurting humanity. These two catalytic ingredients provide the synergy for real revival at your house.

When Mary and Martha can live at peace in the same house, *you can call for Jesus and He'll raise your dead brothers*!

Saul began his spiritual journey as a devoted Martha doing evil works in God's name. Throughout church history, misled religious zealots have believed they were doing God's work by killing people who didn't think or worship the way they believed they should. Saul thought he was doing good, and that is why God honored his motives while firmly confronting his evil deeds. All it took was a 30-second Mary encounter with the risen Christ to transform Saul the misled Martha into Paul the Mary.

Our biggest challenge is learning how to move smoothly between the two. Have you ever gone through seasons in your life when you tended to lean more toward Mary's life of worship or more toward Martha's life of service?

Seasons have come in my life when I knew God was birthing something in my spirit. Although I have a natural liking for management, I found that I just didn't want to be bothered or distracted with the endless details of the ministry office or the practical details of ministry and home life. At other times, God has led me beyond the prayer closet and positions of worship to compassionate service and ministry to the needs of other people.

TAKING SMALL JOURNEYS TO THE OTHER SIDE

Every three months or so, many of us seem to experience small journeys to the other side of life when we feel more passionate about one side than about the other. I've also noticed that God seems to lead us into longer seasons that may span five-to-seven year cycles. I believe He sends us on these trips to the other side to accomplish a deeper work in us that is related to specific purposes in the Kingdom or in our personal lives.

If you are Martha experiencing a new and burning desire to be Mary, then "go for it" with all of your heart. If you are a Mary feeling an odd leaning toward the compassionate service of Martha, then serve and minister to people as if you are serving God.[15] Don't be surprised if God adds some lasting balance to your life along the way.

Jesus called the process "denying yourself and taking up your cross daily."[16] Paul called it "being conformed to the image of Christ."[17] They are one and the same thing—God is determined to balance us horizontally and vertically to match the Christlike dimensions of the cross of discipleship.

HIS POWER WORKS BEST IN YOUR WEAKNESS

Regardless of where we begin the process—as a Mary or as a Martha—we move into new seasons when we are exposed to the hunger of God and begin to worship.

It is in the middle of our weaknesses that the God who dwells in us is most revealed or "made strong" in our lives. I read somewhere that God told Paul, "My gracious favor is all you need. My power works best in your weakness."[18]

Martha leans harder on the strength and provision of God when she finds herself in the place of prayer, praise, worship, and spiritual service. Her discomfort and insufficiency drives her closer to the Rock of her life.

Even Mary seeks His face more fervently when she is moved beyond the comfortable surroundings of the prayer room. She feels the sharp pangs of love and adoration even more when circumstance pulls her away from private communion with her Beloved to serve others in His name in practical ways.

Balance comes to our lives and the Church when Marthas begin to worship and Marys begin to serve. Again, I think that it is probably as much an epiphany for Mary to have a spiritual encounter while in the kitchen as it is for Martha to have a spiritual encounter at His feet. It was Jesus who said, "As you did it to one of the least of these My brethren, you did it to Me."[19]

Intimidation may be our greatest obstacle during these trips to the other side. It can be overwhelming for a Martha to wander into a prayer room filled with worshiping Marys, and the same is true for Marys who wander into a busy kitchen while still wiping away their tears from an intimate encounter with Him.

Martha must not intimidate Mary and push her out of the kitchen before God has accomplished His purposes in the visit. In most cases, Mary will never match the skill and efficiency of Martha in the kitchen, but she *can* fulfill God's perfect will in that place by serving faithfully until He tells her to return to her place of service in prayer and worship.

WHISPERING TO GOD UNDER THE PIANO AGAIN

Mary must never intimidate Martha out of the prayer room. Sometimes I enter prayer meetings and feel intimidated by the overwhelming volume and passion of the people praying there. I tend to preach a great deal about serving God with passion, but when it comes to intimate prayer, the Lord and I just have a good talk. (I'm sure most people wouldn't be very impressed if they were to eavesdrop on our conversations together.) In those awkward moments, I just want to crawl under a table or piano somewhere and whisper to Him. Why? I feel intimidated.

Somehow we must learn to override the intimidation factor so we can fulfill God's will for our lives whether we find ourselves in Martha's kitchen or Mary's prayer corner. Jesus was always shifting back and forth between the spiritual and the natural. If we ever want to seriously impact our world, we must learn how to make that the transition from the spiritual into the natural. Brother Lawrence, for example, refused to draw a line between the sacred and the secular. He called washing dishes "worship" in his classic

15th century book, *Practicing the Presence of God*. The writings of the humble "dish washer" have influenced multiple generations to chase God fervently while serving man faithfully.

David said, "You know when I sit and when I rise; You perceive my thoughts from afar. You discern my going out and my lying down; You are familiar with all my ways."[20] There will be times of both. You must learn to make an easy transition between the spiritual and the supernatural without going from "glory" to "goofy."

Jesus felt comfortable in one particular house in Bethany because Mary entertained His divinity and Martha hosted His humanity. God is confronting us with a paradigm shift. He wants both Mary and Martha in His house.

> *Lord, help us to be more sensitive in the times and the seasons when You knock at our door. Help us to know when to pray as Mary and when to serve as Martha. We desperately need Your wisdom to strike the balance between the two so You will feel comfortable among us. In the meantime, Lord, we willingly live in the tension between Mary and Martha while living and working together to host Your presence.*

Endnotes

1. You may not feel that my friends faced any real risk at all, but you will see that is precisely my point. Although my doctor friend may feel perfectly comfortable conducting complex medical procedures on a living patient, you may not. I doubt that the Lord will ask you to perform medical procedures without a license to practice medicine, but He is almost certain to move you into a situation where obedience requires you to face a faith-stretching risk of some kind.

2. Tommy Tenney, *The God Catchers* (Nashville, TN: Thomas Nelson Publishers, 2000), p. 65.

3. See Romans 8:29.

4. 1 John 3:16.

5. See John 12:4-6.

6. See Acts 6:5–7:60.

7. See Matthew 26:40.

8. See John 18:10; Luke 22:49-51; Matthew 26:52. For a complete exegesis of this passage, read *God's Secret to Greatness: The Power of the Towel* (Ventura, CA: Regal Books, a division of Gospel Light, 2000).

9. See Matthew 26:33-35,69-75.

10. See Acts 1:13-14; 2:1-4,13-16,36-41.

11. See Acts 10:9-20.

12. See Galatians 2:11-14.

13. See John 21:15-17.

14. The apostle Peter wrote First and Second Peter as epistles or letters to the churches.

15. See Ephesians 6:5-8.

16. See Luke 9:23.

17. See Romans 8:29.

18. 2 Corinthians 12:9, *New Living Translation*.

19. Matthew 25:40.

20. Psalm 139:2-3 NIV.

Chapter Eight

THE PRIORITY OF HIS PRESENCE

When Do We Serve? When Do We Worship?

Most of us find it hard to believe that the "God of More Than Enough" doesn't have enough of His two most treasured commodities, but it's true. God isn't really concerned about a shortage of house maintenance workers because He has a whole house full of people who are willing to "work the work of His hands" in the house. He doesn't have any problems in Heaven's kitchen either—a lot of people feel called to the oven and the popular job of food preparation for the family.

The shortage shows up in two key areas of God's economy that just aren't as popular or as easily done as the housework of Divinity.

The first shortage is so crucial that the Father Himself has taken to the streets in search of a solution. Even though this is an "in-house" shortage, the need is so great that God is personally conducting a divine search *for people who will worship Him.*[1]

Our Father went to the "byways" because He often has a house full of Marthas who think it is Mary's job to handle all the "praying and spiritual stuff," much as a private serving in the Army motor pool thinks "all that fighting stuff" is for the infantrymen in the field.

It doesn't dawn on him that he is a soldier first and an Army diesel mechanic second.

The second shortage is linked to the first. A shortage of worship always produces a *shortage of workers* as well, for the greatest works of God are fueled by the intimate relationship that is only birthed in worship.

The shortage of field hands is so critical that Jesus commanded us to pray to the Lord of the harvest for more *reapers* to work in the field of souls.[2] The problem here is that no one wants to "go outside" of the comfortable kitchen in the house of God to work the fields. Could it be that His house is full but His fields are empty? It takes the passion of God in human hearts to propel them beyond the comforts of home and church to do anointed works of compassion. True worship doesn't encourage isolationism; it fosters divine impartation of the passion of God for the lost and hurting world.

There are plenty of people who will work the work of His hands, but God is trying to move us all to a seat at His feet when He visits us—even if it isn't our place of primary service. He knows He will never lack for field hands if we place our lives in His hands. We've already looked at Martha's apparent choice to sit in the kitchen rather than sit at His feet, but she appeared to get over that.

IT WAS JUDAS WHO OBJECTED TO MARY'S WORSHIP IN SIMON'S HOUSE

The dichotomy between earthly viewpoints and heavenly perspectives became especially clear the night Mary broke the alabaster box and anointed Jesus in the house of Simon the leper. We find Martha serving in the kitchen once again, but we hear no voice of complaint from her this time. Her heart rejoiced in Mary's gift to the One who raised their dead brother, Lazarus. It was Judas, the betrayer in waiting, who objected to Mary's worship that night.

When Judas Iscariot asked why the fragrant oil wasn't sold and given to the poor, he prioritized the poor above the presence of Divinity (and some of the others joined in agreement).[3] Jesus interrupted them, told the men to leave Mary alone, and said, "You will always have the poor among you, but you will not always have Me."[4] In other words, He told them, "There are times when you need to feed the poor, but right now *My presence is the priority*."

Martha had already received the lesson Jesus was teaching the people at the feast: When the Master is in the house, you must set aside all other pursuits for the pursuit that matters most—to sit at His feet and seek His face. When Jesus comes to visit the church, the meeting point for all of us—Marthas and Marys alike—is in worship.

I heard my father say one time, "The last days will bring out either the best in you or the worst in you, and you determine that." The same atmosphere that brought out the best in Mary also brought out the worst in Judas. He criticized Mary's selfless gift as selfish, and when he belittled the need to anoint Jesus with such expensive oil, he was saying, in effect, "What a waste—He isn't worth it!"

The fires of persecution were roaring through Jerusalem and Judea. Pressure was mounting in the halls of religious orthodoxy to "do something" about Jesus and His miracles. The disciples found it harder to blend in because the One they followed stood out from the crowd even more as the day of His victory grew nearer.

THIS PASSOVER WOULD CHANGE ALL OTHERS

The resurrection of Lazarus had crossed the line for the Lord's enemies in the Sanhedrin, and rumors of murder and intrigue trickled through Jerusalem as the great feast of Passover approached.[5] Mary and Judas both sensed the pressure, and they knew that *this Passover* would change all others.

With the pressure of Jesus' last days mounting daily, Judas and Mary found themselves in the same house, in the same room, at the same feast. Judas must have wrestled with feelings of jealousy and envy over the privileged place Mary's passionate worship had carved in Jesus' heart. The stress and notoriety of Lazarus' death and resurrection by Jesus had only drawn Mary closer to Him in recent days (while pushing Judas farther out of the picture).

It is likely that Judas resented Mary's presence at the banquet any-way. This was Simon's house, not hers. The traditions of the day didn't favor single women leaving the kitchen to join men in public banquets unless they were the wrong kind of women brought in for all of the wrong reasons.[6] Yet there she was, wiping His feet *with her hair!*[7]

When you feel the impending pressure of His presence or of the crushing weight of adverse circumstance, your brokenness will pro-duce bitterness or sweetness, cursing or praise, burning cynicism or unspeakable joy. It is up to you whether pressure brings out your best or your worst.

PRESSURE CRUSHED THE BRITTLE SOUL OF JUDAS

As the sweet fragrance of Mary's worship filled the room, a brood-ing envy filled Judas' heart and spilled out of his mouth. Pressure crushed the brittle soul of Judas and produced a bitter broth: "You should have sold that oil and given the money to the poor."

The same pressure harvested the nectar of Mary's brokenness and passion to produce a drink God said we would never forget. Mary must have thought to herself, *It's either now or never; I have to give it to Him before it's too late.*

Mary sensed His days on earth were numbered, and she refused to miss the moment. "If I don't pour oil on Him now, no one is going to do it when He dies." The cost of her sacrifice wasn't even a con-sideration; but for bitter Judas, money was everything. "Well, we don't have that in our budget." Passion will cause you to do things that logic says you can't afford.

Pressure in the spirit realm continues to mount in *our day* as well. It will cause some to grow more distracted and entangled in the doing of "things" rather than in the pursuit of God. We see instant "replays" of the scene in Luke 10:40 every day in our churches, and God is saying, "Martha, Martha, you are worried and troubled about many things." He wants us to choose the *one thing* and *best part* that we need more than any other.[8] The problem is that we choose it less than any other.

Most of the Church feels more comfortable with Martha's "pre-meditated preparations" for worship rather than with the act of

worship itself. Both are important, but worship is far more important than preparations for worship. We shouldn't choose between
the two—we are called to both. God wants Mary *and* Martha serving
in His house.

DROP THE PREPARATIONS AND PRAISE HIM WHEN HE COMES

We are careful to prepare our houses of worship before every corporate gathering. We design our services and work out the details of
their order and content in advance. This is Martha serving God at her
best, and it is of great value in the proper time and place. Our mistake,
as that of Martha before us, is our failure to drop the preparations and
sit at His feet when His manifest presence arrives. We must learn to
stop preparing and start praising Him when He shows up.

Should we spend every moment of every service worshiping at
the altar? It sounds good in an idealistic way, but it seems impracti-
cal and impossible this side of Heaven. The fact is that our practical
God provided preaching, teaching, exhortation, and the gifts to help
equip us for the work of the ministry.[9] (Was Paul bringing up that incon-
venient "harvest" thing again?)

If the pattern demonstrated in the Acts of the Apostles and
taught throughout the Epistles means anything, then we have *work*
to do on earth while we worship God who is Spirit. As long as we
live in a world with one unsaved soul, we will need anointed
Marthas to work alongside anointed Marys.

In God's view, we should have no problem moving smoothly
from the natural to the supernatural and vice versa. He has made us
spiritual "amphibians," equipped to breathe the air of His presence
one moment and take His life into the smoky and polluted realm of
man and the natural realm in the next.

The problem plaguing our services is simple: We must become
sensitive enough to know when His *manifested presence* enters our
meetings and adjust accordingly.

I described the difference between the omnipresence of God and
His manifest presence in *The God Chasers*:

The phrase, "omnipresence of God," refers to the fact that He is everywhere all the time. He is that "particle" in the atomic nucleus that nuclear physicists cannot see and can only track. The Gospel of John touches on this quality of God when it says, "And without Him was not any thing made that was made" (Jn. 1:3b).

...This explains why people can sit on a bar stool in an inebriated state and suddenly feel the conviction of the Holy Spirit without the benefit of a preacher, gospel music, or any other Christian influence.

...Yet even though God is everywhere all the time, there are also times when He *concentrates* the very essence of His being into what many call "the manifest presence of God." When this happens, there is a strong sense and awareness that God Himself has "entered the room." You might say that although He is indeed everywhere all the time, there are also specific periods of time when He is "here" *more* than "there."[10]

The omnipresence of God permeated the wilderness when Moses was still herding his father-in-law's sheep in the wilderness, but the children of Israel still suffered under Pharaoh's brutality. It took God's concentrated or manifested presence in the burning bush to arrest the attention of Moses and launch the rescue of Israel from Egyptian bondage.[11]

IT TOOK THE MANIFESTED PRESENCE OF GOD TO TRANSFORM SAUL INTO PAUL

God was "everywhere" when Saul went to Damascus to persecute Christians, but the Pharisee was still convinced he was doing God a favor by stamping out the renegade Jewish sect called Christians. It took the manifested presence of God on a single spot beside the road to strike down and transform Saul the murderer into Paul the martyr for Christ.[12]

These are just two examples of people who recognized God's presence and honored Him by offering Him their lives. I'm convinced that God often visits our meetings, especially when we begin to forget about ourselves and focus upon Him. Yet we rarely acknowledge His manifest presence. Even less often do we honor God by offering Him complete control of our agendas and our lives.

Have you ever visited a friend or relative who makes you feel that your visit is an inconvenience or a disruption in their smoothly flowing and entirely predictable daily schedule? I've visited with people who acted like I wasn't even there. I just wanted to lead them out of the kitchen by the hand and say, "Would you come in here and sit down and talk to me?"

"Well, I'm sorry, I have to go finish this."

Meanwhile I was thinking, *I came to visit and spend some time with you, but all you want to do is clean and cook. If you really valued my time, you would have taken care of this before I got here.* Here are some typical examples that seem to show up in everyone's life—only the names are changed to identify the guilty:

> One lady used to whisk any "dirty" plates right from underneath my nose the moment I lifted the final bite of sandwich, salad, or dessert from the plate. I got the feeling she was anticipating the second I'd let go of my fork, hoping to snag it before a crumb dropped on her spotless tablecloth.

> Another friend followed a rigid schedule of rising, dining, exercise, and bedtime. If you missed the preset mealtime, the unwritten rule (seemingly modeled on boarding house rules) was that you had to wait until the next scheduled "feeding time." If your visit happened to stretch past the magical hour of her bedtime, her eyes would glaze over and she would suddenly stand without notice to announce that she was going to bed. On her way out of the room, she would ask that the last one out turn off the lights and lock the door. She refused to allow anything or anyone disrupt her schedule, even a much-anticipated visitation.

> The "plastic" family greets you at the door with a request that you leave your shoes outside and politely point to the plastic

runners lining all the major traffic ways through their house. The living room and dining room are filled with wonderful furniture, costly china, and hundreds of delicate knickknacks (a nightmare for any family with kids). The feature you remember best is the odd crackling sound you heard every time you sat down on their furniture—it was the plastic covering that graced every seat, sofa, loveseat, and chair in the house. Even the mattresses in the bedrooms boasted fitted plastic slipcovers to protect them from accidents and to provide unforgettable "sound bytes" for guests fortunate enough to spend the night.

The friend whose most prized possession is his electric vacuum appears with vacuum in hand at the first hint of your leaving, so you say to yourself, "Really, I don't need much of a hint. I think it's time to go." Before you can get to your feet, the house is filled with the hum of the vacuum, so you have to raise your voice just to say your good-byes. If you don't move fast enough, he may ask you to lift your feet while he whisks over his primary target zone, the place where you and your family were sitting.

These wonderful characters in our lives rarely mean anything by their antics, but you get the feeling that they don't really value your presence as much as you wish they would. Jesus may have felt this way during the first incident involving Mary and Martha in Bethany. Perhaps that is why Jesus told Martha, in essence, "Right now there is one priority and that is what you need to do. You need to be in here with Me, Martha; the food, the drinks, and the dishes can wait. I want you to spend time with Me."[13]

PUT UP THE VACUUM CLEANER— HE ISN'T FINISHED WITH YOU YET

Consider for a moment how the Holy Spirit feels when we respond to the fresh breeze of His presence moving in our service with a statement such as, "And now we move on to the next part of the service." What did we do? We just pulled out our vacuum cleaner. By our actions we tell the Holy Spirit of God, "Well, we're glad You dropped by. Here's Your hat, but don't be in a hurry to leave. We'll just work around You...."

What an incredible dichotomy! On one hand we say, "O come, Holy Spirit. Come and manifest Your presence among us." When He comes, we say, "I hope You didn't plan on staying too long. We have roasts in the oven, first-time visitors in the congregation, and agendas to follow." We fail to turn divine visitation into holy habitation because we don't value His presence. The solution is simple: "Martha, when His presence is in the house, you take off your apron, come out of the kitchen, and sit at His feet."

We honor God by prioritizing His presence over our preparations for His presence. It all comes down to choices.

> *"We fail to turn divine visitation into holy habitation because we don't value His presence."*

Many people have a popular feature on their home telephone system called "call waiting." You may be in the middle of a conversation when a little beep interrupts you mid-sentence and confronts you with a decision of priorities: Do you offend the person on the first line by asking them to wait "on hold" while you talk to someone on line two who is obviously more important to you? If you ignore the incoming call and carry on your conversation, you might be missing the call of your spouse, your mother, your stranded child, the President of the United States, or most likely, a telemarketing call.

JESUS IS SAYING, "DON'T PUT ME ON HOLD!"

Jesus was trying to tell Martha, "Don't put Me on hold. I am the priority." He's trying to tell us the same thing today. If you are driving down the road and you sense the presence of the Lord enter the car, what do you do? Do you tell the King of Glory, "I'll get back with You later, Lord"? I think I would stop the car and tend to the call of Divinity. Everything else can wait.

At times I've sensed the presence of God enter a service right in the middle of my message and I knew I faced a choice. I could say, "I need to follow my notes," or I could tell myself, "It's time to choose the best part, the one thing that really matters—I need to follow Him."

Life consists of daily decisions and continual choices because it is Divinity's design for humanity. The first hint of it shows up in Genesis, the book of beginnings. If you examine the first two chapters of Genesis, you will notice that the tree of the knowledge of good and evil (the one with the forbidden fruit) was in the *middle* of the garden so Adam and Eve had to pass it every day. It forced them to prioritize God every day.

If the garden layout had been delegated to you or me, we would put the tree back in the corner and shielded it with a wall of briars and brambles so that the choice to avoid sin wouldn't be so hard. Adam and Eve would have been forced to go out of their way to eat fruit from the one forbidden tree in the garden.

God doesn't seem to think that way. The Book of Genesis describes how God created, made, or formed every living thing and commanded them to function and flourish. He decreed the general positions of the land, the seas, and the heavens and made every tree grow out of the ground. Then the Bible pointedly describes how God carefully positioned two trees in the *middle* of the garden for divine purpose.[14] In other words, it was no accident. God did it *on purpose*.

CHOOSE ME *EVERY* DAY

I can almost hear Him tell the puzzled angels watching the creation spectacle, "I want them right *there*—right in the middle of My garden." When the angels asked Him why, He might have said, "Because I want the creatures created in My image to pass by them every day. That way they will have to choose Me and My tree of life over their desire for the forbidden fruit." I remember reading somewhere, "*Choose you this day....*"[15] Perhaps we should recast this command in the light of Jesus' statement about taking up our cross daily: "Choose you *every* day."[16]

Satan looks for opportunities to interfere with our lives through the gate of our wrong choices and misplaced priorities. For example, consider the two great commandments Jesus quoted in the Gospels:

> *"You shall love the Lord your God with all your heart, with all your soul, and with all your mind." This is the first and great commandment. And the second is like it: "You shall love your neighbor as yourself."*[17]

The devil's first choice would be to make you stop obeying either one of these commandments. If that doesn't work, then he will settle for inverting their God-given priority by moving the second-best thing ahead of the very best. He hopes to rob you of the power of the moment by keeping your focus on yourself or your neighbor when you should be looking at the Master. If he succeeds, he can steal or prevent all of the miraculous works divine visitation would accomplish in your life.

DROP YOUR DISHTOWEL, MARTHA— IT'S TIME TO WORSHIP HIM!

Ideally, the minute we sense His presence enter our meetings, we all would drop our dishtowels and say, "Okay, that's it. We can take care of the preparations later—the One we've been looking for is here. It's time to listen to the Lord and bless Him." Unfortunately, that also is the time the Martha in us wants to hop up and get busy.

So how do you know when to serve with Martha and when to drop everything and sit at His feet with Mary? The solution is simple: When He is in the house, don't do anything but entertain Him. Throw out your agenda and take the "Mary position" at His feet.

Anticipate His coming (after all, that is what Martha *prepared* for) by watching for it in your church services and in your personal devotional times. Watch and wait for His presence to appear at every opportunity. You may feel like you are going through the motions when you begin to praise Him, but worship by faith while you ignore your protesting body and weary mind. The sacrifice of praise will be worth it when you sense an uplifting breeze of the Holy Spirit or taste the sweetness of His presence as He enters the room.

Take extra care not to grieve the Holy Spirit. Paul warned us, "And do not grieve the Holy Spirit of God, by whom you were sealed for the day of redemption" and "Do not quench the Spirit."[18]

HOW TO LEARN THE ART OF HOSTING THE HOLY GHOST

How do we honor God's presence without grieving the Holy Spirit? If you want to understand the art of hosting the Holy Ghost, just watch someone carry around a dove.

My mom and dad went on an overseas trip when I was about 18 years old and in college. On a whim, I decided to buy Mom a white dove as a homecoming gift. She fell in love with it and decided, for some reason, to name that dove Fletcher.

I've never seen another dove like Fletcher. He became so "hand tamed" that he would lie on his back and let us scratch his belly. Each morning when Mom got up to make coffee (a time-honored Louisiana practice), Fletcher would coo and make other kinds of noises until she released him from his cage. He liked to sit on her shoulder as she drank coffee, and sometimes he would sit on a rim of the saucer and drink coffee with her. This bird was irrationally tame! Yet as tame as Fletcher was, he was very particular about how we moved in his presence.

I learned that I had to hold still if I wanted him to fly to me. When Fletcher was perched on my shoulder or hand, he would fly away if I made fast movements or even changed directions too quickly. With practice, we all learned how to move through the house with Fletcher perched on a shoulder or hand, but *we had to learn how to walk*. (The Bible calls it walking "circumspectly."[19])

A CONTROLLING GRIP CAN GRIEVE AND QUENCH THE HOLY SPIRIT

All four Gospel accounts say the Holy Spirit is "like a dove."[20] If you could picture people in the church carrying a dove, you would see some people carrying it with an open palm and allowing the dove to perch where and when he chooses. Many of them, though, would revert to their usual practice in life and enclose the dove in their tight fists to "hold on to it." This describes how many of us try to "carry" the Holy Spirit. We want to "hold onto" God with such a grip that we grieve and quench the Holy Spirit in the process.

In the natural, if you try to hold a dove with a tight grip, you will kill it. On the other hand, if you can ever learn to carry the dove gently, he will contentedly perch on your hand or shoulder even while you go from place to place. We must learn to entertain or host the Holy Ghost in our homes, church services, and even on the streets of our cities.

Somehow Mary and Martha developed such an ability to host the dual-natured Savior that He preferred to stay in their home rather than the finest homes and inns of Jerusalem. God is still looking for more Bethanys. He is looking for a place where both Mary and Martha are waiting to serve Divinity and humanity with sensitivity and purity of heart. Does your house or church qualify?

When He is in the house, Martha must come out of the kitchen and join Mary at His feet. When His manifest presence is not there, Mary must be willing to join Martha in the kitchen to prepare for His coming and to exercise godly compassion toward humanity. *The difficulty comes when we try to move smoothly between the kitchen and the altar.*

The Lord made this especially real during a special meeting I called to launch the writing of this book. About 50 people felt led to join me in Louisiana on short notice so that I could share with them these ideas I had on my heart concerning Mary, Martha, and the Church. In the middle of the session in which we covered the specific points in this chapter, I sensed the Holy Spirit was putting me to the test. He seemed to say to me, "Do you want to keep talking about this book, or do you want to allow Me to land every once in awhile?" We immediately dropped the meeting agenda so we could turn our attention solely to God.

Don't be surprised if the Holy Spirit interrupts you while you read this book. That is your cue to lay down this book, take off your serving apron, and lay down your heart before God in worship.

Endnotes

1. See John 4:23.

2. See Matthew 9:37-38; Luke 10:2.

3. See Matthew 26:6-11; Mark 14:3-7; John 12:1-8.

4. John 12:8 NIV.

5. See John 11:43-57.

6. The Gospels demonstrate by context and setting that Mary's actions in Simon's house were entirely virtuous, but Judas didn't have the benefit of hindsight. He was seeing everything through the filter of bitterness and self-hatred. He would naturally want to think the worst, especially toward someone he viewed as competition for the Lord's approval. Kathleen E. Corley, in *Private Women, Public Meals: Social Conflict in the Synoptic Tradition* (Peabody, MA: Hendrickson Publishers, Inc., 1993), indicates that respectable women rarely dined in public settings, and when they did so, they were accompanied by their husbands. In both Greco-Roman and ancient Near-Eastern literature, public banquets attended by women with expensive *alabastron* or alabaster containers of anointing oil were generally connected with prostitution or promiscuous behavior (see pages 103-104 in Corley's book). Jesus set the record straight for Judas and anyone else entertaining wrong or critical ideas about Mary's prophetic gift in anticipation of His death.

7. See John 12:3.

8. See Luke 10:41.

9. See Ephesians 4:11-28. This compacted passage describes the wisdom of God for the Church. He supplies ministers to the Church as *equippers*, not as objects of worship or beasts of burden. Their job

is to equip the "average believer" for the supernatural job of ministering to the lost world, and it only can be accomplished as each member does his part to build God's house. Paul quickly takes us from the supernatural to the naturally practical in a way that shows how unity between Mary and Martha is indispensable to the Church.

10. Tommy Tenney, *The God Chasers* (Shippensburg, PA: Destiny Image Publishers, 1998), pp. 36-37.

11. See Exodus 3:2-8. The "Angel of the Lord" in this passage is generally understood to be the pre-incarnate Christ.

12. See Acts 9:1-20.

13. See Luke 10:40-42.

14. See Genesis 2:9.

15. See Joshua 24:15 KJV.

16. Jesus said, "If anyone desires to come after Me, let him deny himself, and take up his cross daily, and follow Me" (Lk. 9:23).

17. Matthew 22:37-39.

18. Ephesians 4:30; 1 Thessalonians 5:19.

19. See Ephesians 5:15.

20. See Matthew 3:16; Mark 1:10; Luke 3:22; John 1:32.

Chapter Nine

CAN YOU RIDE A BICYCLE?

The Art of Navigation by Constant Compensation

Modern society moves at such a hectic pace in many industrialized nations that many believe all you have to do to fall behind is to stand still. We could make a similar statement about the Kingdom of God—all it takes to fall into a ditch is to stop moving. The virtue isn't solely in the movement itself, it is in the constant compensation it makes available.

Do you remember the first time you tried to ride a bicycle? Most of us tackled that project totally unaware of the key to success on those two-wheeled wonders—*you have to keep moving*.

Our untrained instincts told us to stop all motion in a time of crisis. Unfortunately, the moment we stopped moving forward we also lost our power to compensate for the bicycle's odd tendency to fall over when the wheels stop rolling. It wasn't until we managed to keep moving through a crisis that we discovered how to avoid a fall by compensating with a turn of the handlebars.

What happened? We learned how to *compensate* when the bike began to lean too far to one side. We're still learning that lesson in our pursuit of His presence.

My colorful childhood memories from the circus still provide my clearest example of "constant compensation." Have you ever watched "high wire" acts in a circus or on television? Did you notice that the artists *stay in motion and keep their arms or balance poles poised for compensation* no matter what form the act takes—whether the person walks across a high wire, rides across the wire on a bicycle or motorcycle, or even crosses the abyss of our imaginations on a unicycle with three people on his shoulders!

DISASTER FOLLOWS A FAILURE TO COMPENSATE

Life and death and success and failure balance precariously on the performer's ability to compensate for every minute's shift of gravity. All it takes for a disastrous fall is the failure to compensate for imbalances.

The same principles apply to your life in Christ. God graciously causes us to compensate for course deviations or imbalances in our lives, but trouble comes when we lose the ability to hear or when we refuse to obey His voice.

Many times we ask for *too much* too quickly from our heavenly Father. We pray for this great spiritual power and then grow rebellious when He says, "You are not ready for it. You don't have the balance required to successfully handle this gift."

The Church is in a constant unbalanced state, and so are you if you can admit it. Why would I say such a thing? It is part of God's design. If we were perfectly balanced in life and ministry, we would be tempted to dismiss our constant need for God's stabilizing grace and mercy—and every Mary or Martha who is on "the other side" of our comfort zone.

We often look to the first-century Church as a picture of God's perfect will for Church operations in the world. The Church described in the Book of Acts and the Epistles really is a good example, but not because of its perfection. We learn more from the early Church's Spirit-led *compensation* and adaptation to changing needs than from its questionable perfection.

The New Testament Church was birthed in an explosive upper room encounter with the presence of God. That encounter transformed the 120 God Chasers into radical God Catchers who were filled with such zeal and power that their testimony and ministry brought thousands into God's Kingdom in one day.[1] Yet they became so "spiritual" that the Bible says the more practical "Martha ministry" to the non-Jewish widows in the congregation was neglected.[2]

The apostles' hair still smelled of smoke from the upper room when the complaints brought them back down to earth in a hurry. The non-Jewish believers told the predominately Jewish leaders, "You know, before we had this great revival and before everybody's hair caught on fire, they used to take care of us widows. Now everybody's so spiritual that all they want to do is dance around, pray, and preach in the streets. They don't even pay attention to us anymore."

GOD GAVE A MARTHA ANOINTING TO 12 MARYS

The 12 apostles knew the problem was real, but they also knew what God had called them to do in that critical window of time. Their only solution was to make a godly *compensation* to restore balance in the Church.

It seems that they decided to find gifted Marthas to look after the business of meeting the widows' needs so the apostles could devote themselves to their Mary calling of prayer and the ministry of the Word.

It is interesting to me that the qualifications for the first deacons or table waiters are similar to a Mary's qualifications. The apostles worded their want ad this way (I think this ad is a permanent fixture in church lobbies and newsletters—I've seen it posted in nearly every church I've been to over the last three decades):

Wanted:
"Seven men of good reputation, full of the Holy Spirit and wisdom, whom we may appoint over this business."[3]

The apostles weren't being prideful or prejudiced against the Martha ministry; they knew the price Jesus had paid to prepare them for that window of time in human history. They really couldn't afford to be distracted from what *they* were supposed to do just so they could do something *someone else* was supposed to do.

Perhaps you've read Paul's description of the situation: "From Him [Christ] the whole body, joined and held together by every supporting ligament, grows and builds itself up in love, as each part does its work."[4]

Countless numbers of men in my "middle-age" bracket are in the season of life when their greatest area of productivity seems to be the space above the belt and below the chin. The new "growth" in extra stomach fat puts quite a strain on the lower back.

As Iron Sharpens Iron, Mary and Martha Sharpen Each Other

Inevitably these men hear a doctor, health trainer, or their wives remind them that the best way to strengthen the back and alleviate back pain is to do *abdominal* exercises. Even if they insist on spelling that "a-b-o-m-i-n-a-b-l-e exercises," it doesn't change the odd fact that the abdomen is on the *opposite* side of the trunk of the body from where they feel lower back pain. Even human physiology seems to follow the biblical wisdom that says, "As iron sharpens iron, so a man sharpens the countenance of his friend."[5]

When the apostles received the complaint about the neglected widows, they faced a situation where Marys and Marthas in the church needed to do their part at the same time to get the job done. This was also the situation at Simon's house during the final meal in Bethany. Martha was serving the Lord from her position in the kitchen while her sister Mary served Him from her position at His feet.[6] Opposites attract Him!

At other times, such as during the time of "tarrying" in the upper room, everyone was called to leave their various " kitchen duties" to assume the Mary position and wait upon or minister to the Lord until He was ready to pour out His blessing upon them.[7]

The apostles solved the problem by appointing anointed Marthas or deacons to take care of serving the tables of the widows while preserving the priority of their apostolic responsibilities.[8]

It seems to me the apostles "elevated the office" of the first deacons and gave honor where honor was due. The apostles clearly viewed the Martha office of table waiting as a supernatural assignment requiring supernatural gifting—it just wasn't *their* primary calling. *Many of our problems stem from the lack of respect we have for anyone who does not have the same ministry and preferences we have.*

NEVER PUT POWER IN THE HANDS OF IMMATURITY

Why did the apostles take such care when choosing deacons or selecting an apostolic replacement for Judas Iscariot? The Scriptures warn us, "Do not lay hands on anyone hastily."[9] That means you should *never put power in the hands of the immature*. If you do, you will pay a high price for it later.

During one meeting, I teased my middle daughter by announcing to the audience, "I want to serve notice to all drivers in the central Louisiana area: My daughter passed her written driver's exam and we are about to empower her with a 2,000-pound automobile." Why would I say something like that? Like any thinking parent of a teenage driver, I have a healthy concern that she may run over something in the process of gaining experience.

My children are well behaved, thoughtful, and responsible; but I have enough common sense to know that won't automatically transform them from new drivers to *experienced* drivers overnight.

Power, strength, and authority in the hands of the immature is dangerous. The ability to handle these responsibly comes over a period of time through a process of learning that includes instruction and extensive trial and error. (It's the "error" part that worries parents of young drivers.)

ACQUIRING THE ACCUMULATED SKILLS OF CONSTANT COMPENSATION

The difference between new drivers and experienced drivers is the accumulated skill of *constant compensation*. Seasoned drivers automatically compensate for subtle changes in speed, direction, and changing traffic and road conditions. Some new drivers aren't even sure where the brake is without looking down.

Have you ever noticed that experienced drivers constantly compensate their course with small subtle movements of the steering wheel to keep the vehicle between the ditches? Only immaturity grips the wheel and statically points the car unswervingly. Unbending inflexibility will land you in a ditch. (Beware the dangers of overcompensation as well—compensate using small movements!)

Sometimes we beg for things God knows we shouldn't have. Have you ever wondered why Jesus called James and John the "sons of thunder"?[10] Perhaps we have the answer in this Gospel passage:

> *And when His disciples James and John saw* [a Samaritan village reject Jesus], *they said, "Lord, do You want us to command fire to come down from heaven and consume them, just as Elijah did?" But He turned and rebuked them, and said, "You do not know what manner of spirit you are of. For the Son of Man did not come to destroy men's lives but to save them."*[11]

They were saying, "Well, Lord, we went in there and they didn't treat us right at that restaurant. They didn't want to serve us in the village, so we'll just revoke their lease on life—just give us the word and the power to do it."

The Lord was saying, in essence, "So that's what you think I came to do? Do you think you should kill everyone who doesn't treat you right? You don't know what kind of spirit is speaking through you."

When we ask for power and authority and don't receive them in the measure we hoped for, it is usually because we're not ready to handle those things at that level. When we read about the miracles occurring through the lives of the apostles, we sometimes pray,

"Okay, Lord, I want power to heal the sick and raise the dead too. Just send me the entire 'Instant Apostle's Miracle-Working Kit.'"

THE ART OF CONSTANT COMPENSATION MAKES US SAFE

He just shakes His head and says, "I would love to give you that power, but there is another side to that power that I can't place in immature hands. You aren't skilled enough in the art of constant compensation and judgment to be safe."

The apostle Paul demonstrated both sides of supernatural authority when he rebuked a Jewish sorcerer named Bar-Jesus for interfering with the work of the Holy Spirit and declared the man would become blind.[12]

When God gives you the power to loose something, He also gives you the power to bind things.[13] You can speak words of life or death and of blessing or cursing. The authority is from God but the individual judgment and wisdom must be developed in your own heart as you learn to constantly compensate by His Spirit.

God requires balance in His Kingdom, but He isn't interested in static stagnation. He is after the kind of "balance in tension" you find when an acrobat crosses a high wire or balances on an oversized ball or barrel using constant compensation to maintain his balance.

He wants both Mary and Martha at work in His house because comfort only comes when needs are met for both humanity *and* Divinity. Just because He created and called you to major on one thing doesn't give you the right to overlook the necessity of the other—you must validate the godly calling of others who are different from you. That is what the apostles did when they decided to appoint godly men to care for the needy widows so they could devote themselves to prayer and ministry.

PULLED BETWEEN PASSION AND COMPASSION

The Lord helps us compensate for personal and corporate imbalances by "pulling us" back and forth between passion for His divinity and compassion for humanity. Each time we yield to this constant bending back and forth, we have the opportunity to "stumble" across Him and have spiritual passion awakened in our lives. (He loves to bless us when we say yes to His Spirit.)

During the series of meetings, called a book birthing, we held to help finalize the material for this book, I experienced one of those times when the Lord pulled me aside and interrupted my agenda. He wanted to compensate for an oversight in our meetings.

In the middle of a late-morning session, a staff member told me that a local tragedy had occurred in which three small children had perished in a tragic house fire. A dear friend of mine had called to say he wouldn't make the meeting because he and his wife were ministering to the grieving parents.

My heart went out to the hurting parents, but I told the staff member, "I don't know what to do. Time is short, and we need to stay focused on what we're doing here."

Oh God, I Missed You

The next day I walked outside in the cool of the morning just before the meetings were scheduled to resume, and I picked up the newspaper in my driveway. The headlines about the tragic fire riveted my heart. I said, "Oh God, I missed You. There we were talking about Mary and Martha when You tapped me on the shoulder and said, 'Okay, this is what it's all about. Now what are you going to do?'"

The truth is that if you are Martha, you instantly know what to do. If you're Mary, however, you are often at a loss in such situations. Mary doesn't even see "the dishes in the sink" and Martha has trouble looking beyond the sink to see Jesus waiting for her. Our knee-jerk reaction to tragedy is usually limited to someone interrupting a meeting to say, "Let's all stand and pray for this family."

Somehow I knew God wanted something more practical from us this time, so I prayed, "God, I don't know what to do. I can't return the children these people lost in the fire. I don't know them so I can't go to them and put my arm around them." In the end, I contacted my friend and asked, "What do they need? What can I do to help them in practical ways? I don't know this family, but what do they need?"

Sometimes Mary needs to receive advice from Martha and vice versa. During a ministry trip to England, our party rented a minivan that seated 19 people (it was really a small bus the size of a motor home). The size of the thing was significant in itself because the roads in England aren't known for being excessively wide. What really made things challenging was that the English (and Europeans in general) drive on the opposite side of the road than Americans.

Those unfortunate enough to sit on the passenger's side (the *driver's* side in America) had the opportunity of watching just how close we came to disaster in intersection after intersection. When tension and their sense of survival finally overcame their timidity, they would say, "You're a little *close* over here."

At first the warnings backfired because the driver wasn't used to compensating from the "passenger's side" of the road, so we usually veered in the wrong direction to compensate. Finally the skills of compensation rose to meet the challenge and everyone in the minivan appreciated the perspective of the "front-seat driver" assisting the nervous driver behind the wheel.

We Appreciate Backseat Martha When She Keeps Mary From Crashing

At times, Mary or Martha needs to tell her counterpart, "You're a little close on this side of the road." Under normal circumstances, few of us can appreciate a "backseat driver" in vehicles or church situations. Appreciation levels quickly change, however, when Backseat Martha keeps Mary from crashing. By the same token, if Martha can value and be sensitive to Mary's advice and compensate accordingly, then God will use her to help keep Martha's life and ministry in the center of God's purposes.

One of my favorite African-American preachers from the past, the late S.M. Lockridge, used to say, "When you're piling up on one side it's falling down on the other. When your blood pressure is high your bank account is low." His words paint a clear picture of our constant struggle to maintain our balance in the Christian life.

One of the greatest keys to the art of spiritual navigation and constant compensation is to listen to the counsel of those who have different or opposite callings from your own. If you are a Mary or are living in a Mary season, pay close attention when a Martha taps on your shoulder and offers advice about some needed compensation.

In every situation, the best thing you can do is ask the Lord, "What can I do? Where do You want me to be and serve?" Sometimes you also need to ask your "opposite" what you can do.

At times my wife has discussed pressing situations with me, leaving out no detail or subpoint in the process. When she finally finishes sharing her heart, I have asked her in typical male fashion, "What do you want me to *do* about that?" Then she answers, "I don't want you to do anything. I just wanted you to know about it, and I wanted to know that you knew."

COMPENSATE BY ACKNOWLEDGING THE VIEWS OF OTHERS

Like many other husbands, I am so action-oriented that I assume when my wife tells me about a problem or concern, she expects me to "fix" it somehow. That wasn't her goal at all. Sometimes the compensation we need comes through a simple acknowledgment of the needs or viewpoints of others. This is especially true in the Church.

The concept of compensation would be easier for us to accept if it was a one-time occurrence or perhaps a monthly event, but it doesn't work that way. As long as we are alive and in our natural bodies, we can never stop compensating for our shortfalls and overextensions in life. Christian maturity isn't marked by an absence of flaws, mistakes, or blunders; but by quick repentance, acceptance of correction, and appropriate compensation. Experience does tend to help us make fewer mistakes, but mistakes still come.

The interaction of Mary and Martha helps create the proper atmosphere for entertaining Divinity and humanity together. The process of constant compensation works much like a thermostat that regulates the temperature in a home or office. Have you ever noticed that the heater doesn't come on and *stay* on under normal conditions? If it does, chances are the conditions won't be very comfortable. On the other hand, have you ever risen on a cold winter morning to discover that your furnace or heater failed during the night?

THERMOSTATS FULFILL THE FUNCTION OF CONSTANT COMPENSATION

Thermostats were invented precisely because it takes more than simply turning on a furnace or an air conditioner to create and maintain the proper atmosphere in a room. A thermostat establishes a comfortable temperature and then constantly compensates for drops or rises in temperature by activating the heating or cooling systems as needed. In other words, thermostats fulfill the function of constant compensation.

I suspect that it takes a similar effort to create the proper spiritual atmosphere in a church. One month the pastor may stand up and say, "You are doing a great job of worshiping God, but we need to make sure we're feeding the hungry." The next month he may say, "I appreciate your selfless work on the streets and in the shelters, but we need to make sure we're worshiping God with the same zeal." People who don't understand the need for constant compensation may say, "I wish the pastor would make up his mind about what is important."

The issue isn't choosing one priority over the other; it is the need to make constant compensations for changes in interior temperature and exterior or external conditions. When there's panic in the streets, God's people should be so coolly confident that there's dancing and rejoicing in the church (the heat of passion for God has little to do with the heat of emotions in times of crisis). When apathy and cynical depression race across a city after a major employer lays off most of its workforce or closes its local plant, the temperature of joy should rise in the church. I read somewhere, "My grace is sufficient for you, for My strength is made perfect in weakness."[14] It takes constant compensation to maintain the atmosphere of peace, joy, and love in the face of ever-changing external stimuli and conditions.

REMEMBER TO FEED THE PRIORITIES OF YOUR LIFE

Sometimes you lose your balance because you get so busy feeding everybody else that you forget to feed the priorities of your life. "Feeding" God worship and love is the top priority of your life according to the Scriptures.[15] If your marriage covenant with God crumbles and falls, then all of your Martha work will be quickly reduced to nothing but a business. You won't have a home, just a restaurant!

A number of church organizations have built extraordinary hospitals and homeless shelters, but the passion of their original relationship to God has faded. Their members sometimes feel like they are punching a religious time clock and going through the motions of good works without any goal. These churches need to make a compensation in their course to regain the fire of their passion for God.

WILL GOD COME TO YOUR HOUSE WHEN HE IS HUNGRY?

The people in a city may know to go to your church when they are hungry and destitute, but will God come there too when He gets hungry? We know that God gets hungry because of Jesus' answer to the disciples when they came back from a restaurant and offered Him some carryout food at Jacob's well near Sychar in Samaria.[16]

"Here, Jesus, we got You something to eat."

"I'm not hungry; I've already eaten. I had meat to eat that you don't understand."

"What did You eat?"

"Oh, I feasted on the worship of one woman at this well and on the doing of My Father's will. I am satisfied."

When God gets hungry, He dines on worship. Jesus told the woman at the well, "But the hour is coming, and now is, when the true worshipers will worship the Father in spirit and truth; for the Father is seeking such to worship Him."[17] The only thing that the Father actively seeks is worshipers—He already knows where every nugget of gold and every diamond is hidden in the mantle of the earth. The rare commodity is worshipers, not gold or diamonds.

Balance is crucial to Christians who really care about chasing God while serving man. The way God helps us keep that balance is by making constant compensations to our circumstances, which in turn requires us to make compensations in our affections, daily choices, ministry methods, and our attitude toward others.

"When God gets hungry, He dines on worship."

Dad Offered Us Burnt Offerings on Mother's Day Out

When I was growing up, my sister and I knew "the pickings would be slim" every time my mother went on a trip or came down with an illness that thrust Dad into the kitchen. The only thing my dad could ever possibly cook was breakfast, and the only thing I remember him cooking for breakfast was cinnamon toast. (Everything else he made resembled a "burnt offering" more than something from a recognizable food group.)

Every time my sister and I talk about it, we start laughing, because Dad had a peculiar talent for creating "polka-dot" cinnamon toast. Let me explain the process just in case you've never prepared or eaten this "delicacy." First you toast a slice of bread and spread butter or margarine over it. Then you lightly sprinkle some sugar over the top and follow it with an even lighter dusting of ground cinnamon. I doubt that nutritionists include cinnamon toast on their menus, but it has been a long-time favorite with kids.

My dad has a unique ability to apply the cinnamon and sugar in such a way that the two ingredients never seem to combine. In one

bite, you may have a mouth full of melted butter and partially dis-
solved sugar with no hint of cinnamon. In the next bite, you may
have an explosion of powdery cinnamon stimulate your tastebuds
without any of the sweetening influence of sugar.

Dad's cinnamon toast reminded me of a freckled face, square-
framed Dalmatian, and of an odd polka-dot creation delivered on a
plank. My sister and I love Dad with all of our hearts, but the
thought of eating his breakfast creation with big dollops of cinnamon here and sugar mounds there is less than appetizing. Frankly, it
was terrible. At least Dad tried.

One of his other shortcomings is that he can't draw a straight
line. We still have the Cub Scout project he made as a boy. It is some
kind of shelf designed to hang on a wall. It is the only thing he's ever
built with his hands as far as I know, and of course, it is crooked.

As a result of this handyman void around the house, I grew up
Mister Fix-It. My mom trusted me to fix things at the age of 12 and
13, but she would tell Dad, "Now, Tom Fred, don't you fool with
that. Just let Tommy fix it." He couldn't cook, draw, or fix things at
all; but he is an incredibly talented person when it comes to some
other things. The point of the story is that my dad compensates. He
was and is a wonderful father and spiritual mentor.

DAD COMPENSATED WITH A SPIRITUAL FEAST

Dad can't cook, draw a straight line, or fix things with his hands;
but oh, how he can cook up a spiritual feast from God's Word for
hungry souls. He knows how to draw a straight line of godly principles from the front door of the church to the back office where the
offerings are counted. He can draw miracles and loving words out
of God's tool box to fix the broken hearts of God's people or repair
church foundations that are cracking. As I said, Dad compensates.

Sometimes God brings radical compensation to the Church by
making radical compensations in individual lives. Some people
have asked me, "Can a Martha ever become a Mary?" I have to
admit that this is what happened in my life.

I spent an early part of my ministry as the pastor of a local church. I was such a Martha that every aspect of the church service was carefully scripted and orchestrated in advance. If your only exposure to my ministry has been in my later years, then you have no idea how much the Martha mind-set dominated my methods.

When I walked into the church service, I carried a specially prepared "in-service format sheet" in my hand that had been Xeroxed and distributed to everyone who had any part to play in the service. It included a blank space just for my use during the service. I was thinking and "pastoring" throughout the service. I constantly wrote down the names of people I needed to talk to and things I needed to do because when I saw a face or a situation developing during the service, it prompted me to make sure other things were covered.

A God Encounter Changed Me From a Martha Into a Mary

So all I did was "see people" throughout the typical worship service in those days. I grew up in church and ministry and I had received Christ as my Lord and Savior, but God sent a major compensation my way. A God encounter changed me from a Martha into a Mary in one day. He doesn't do this to everyone, but in my case, everything in my life changed once holy hunger overtook my soul and I experienced a God encounter with His face. After that, all I could do was see God everywhere. Now I have to force myself to tend to the Martha duties in my life and ministry.

God permanently changed my appetite and rearranged my priorities, even though they weren't evil or wrongly placed before the encounter. God chose to re-prioritize my world so I could help the Church re-prioritize its ideas about worship. I've noticed He is doing the same thing to other people too. Sometimes He sends transformed Jewish scholars to reach non-Jewish people, and sometimes He sends transformed Marthas to restore the Mary ministry to the Church.

This divine balance between *chasing God* and *serving man* reminds me of the time-honored Louisiana art of making a "roux," a cooked mixture of flour and cooking oil that Southern chefs claim is the basis of all good food. Roux is used as a base and thickening agent for many of the soups and sauces common to Southern and Cajun recipes. The ingredients are few and simple, but the process of mixing them together to form roux is difficult and time-consuming (and only a minority of cooks and chefs have mastered it).

You make roux by browning flour in a skillet with just a little bit of oil. It sounds simple but it takes around 45 minutes to complete the job. If you rush the process you will end up with lumpy roux or, even worse, you'll burn the mixture and be forced to start over.

The art of making roux is so difficult and time-consuming that some seasoned Cajun cooks in fine restaurants buy their roux in jars at the grocery store. It is easier to prepare roux in large commercial batches, and chefs discovered roux can be refrigerated without harming its taste or consistency.

This process of gentle mixing and slow heat reminds me of the way God uses Mary and Martha to constantly compensate for little imbalances between them to create the perfect atmosphere for His presence. Unfortunately, most of us would prefer to purchase the ready-made mix if we could find the prepackaged format in any store or catalog.

The miracle of Bethany occurred because Martha worked in advance to create a place in her home where Jesus' humanity felt comfortable and welcome. This in turn created an opportunity for Mary to sit at His feet and minister to His divinity.

These two complementary gifts also recreated the atmosphere in the house of Simon the leper despite the best efforts of the disciples. Jesus ate a meal prepared by a transformed Martha, but He had to do it while sitting in a room that was full of male Marthas. These untransformed Marthas had not made any compensation for their narrow focus on the natural realm and their own place in it. They seemed to be consumed with worries about the future and about their place in the coming Kingdom.

Then Mary entered and broke her alabaster box of broken worship and adoration to anoint Him for His death. Her sacrifice transformed the atmosphere of the room despite the grumbling and criticism of Judas and his chorus of unchanged Marthas.

The path of the Son from Bethany to the cross was difficult enough as it was. Perhaps the Father made a special compensation by bringing the anointings of both Mary and Martha to Simon's house so Jesus' last meal in Bethany was marked by peace and comfort and balanced ministry to His humanity and His divinity.

What will He find in your house? Will Mary and Martha coexist peacefully? Will your house be a Bethany or another Bethlehem with "no vacancy" for divine visitation?

Endnotes

1. See Acts 2.

2. See Acts 6:1-7.

3. Adapted from Acts 6:3.

4. Ephesians 4:16 NIV.

5. Proverbs 27:17.

6. See John 12:2-3.

7. See Acts 1:13-14.

8. See Acts 6:3-7.

9. 1 Timothy 5:22a.

10. See Mark 3:17.

11. Luke 9:54-56.

12. See Acts 13:6-12.

13. See Matthew 16:19.

14. 2 Corinthians 12:9.

15. See Matthew 22:37-38; John 4:23-24.

16. See John 4:5-42.

17. John 4:23.

Chapter Ten

THE CHURCH IS USUALLY A LITTLE "UNBALANCED"

God's People Can Go From "Glory" to "Goofy"

Although I hope every Christian experiences a genuine encounter with the manifested presence of God, I also realize that even a supernatural encounter *isn't enough* to ignite true revival in a church, a city, or a nation.

We were all born to be God Chasers and therefore, also God Catchers. When He allows us to "catch" Him in private moments or public meetings we are never the same. (Much as David was never the same after worship encounters on the backside of the sheep pasture as a boy, and as a king while building "God's favorite house," the one men call "the tabernacle of David."[1])

Encounters with His presence change us. Yet there is a bigger picture and a greater purpose behind it all. Our God, "who desires all men to be saved," wants more people to come to Him through Jesus Christ, and that brings us to the subject of revival.[2]

What is true revival? Some say all you need for revival is for God to show up. I've also heard revivalists say in previous years, "Give me a crowd of people, and I'll give you revival." (I'm sure they could deliver something, but I'm very sure it wasn't "revival.")

Again, real revival is when both God and man show up at the same time and the same place. That can happen only when you have *credibility in both realms.* You must have enough credibility in the human realm to make man feel comfortable, and you must have credibility in the divine realm to make God feel comfortable.

An attorney who wants to practice law in his home state as well as before the United States Supreme Court must establish credentials in both realms. The high court deals with issues in constitutional law that rarely, if ever, turn up in local courts. The legal arguments and evidence considered acceptable there are entirely different from those used in state and local courts, where state laws and local ordinances are the main concern.

The only way to handle both areas of the law is to acquire specialized knowledge and establish credibility to satisfy both the Supreme Court justices in Washington's realm and the judges of your local state jurisdictions.

When I am invited to other countries, my hosts go to great lengths to find interpreters skilled in English and in the local languages and dialects. That can be quite a challenge in a nation such as India or in Central America where many different languages or local dialects can be found in a single region. If these interpreters lack credibility and ability in both languages, the effectiveness of my ministry in that nation can be seriously compromised.

A skilled interpreter can help bring a spiritual breakthrough to a meeting by making two parties comfortable—they make me feel comfortable and confident through their abilities, and they make the audience happy by accurately conveying the heart of my message.

FIND A DIVINE MODEL FOR BUILDING YOUR HOUSE

If you are serious about preparing a house of habitation where both God and man feel comfortable enough to stay under the same roof, then find a divine model in God's Word and follow it. We know that Mary and Martha managed to make Jesus feel totally comfortable in their house in Bethany. They did it by successfully juggling two seemingly conflicting priorities: *Mary entertained His divinity while Martha entertained His humanity.*

It was through the careful accommodation of two realms that Mary and Martha made their house in Bethany a meeting place where God and man came together in an atmosphere of hospitality and worship. As far as I know, it is the only house mentioned in the New Testament that became the habitual resting place of Jesus.

There was "something right" about Mary and Martha's place that drew God through the door for extended stays. Things haven't really changed. What worked then still works now. We still struggle to find the balance that draws His manifest presence through our doors for extended stays. It seems the Bethany model for turning divine visitation into divine habitation is the only way to really bring the *humanity of your community into contact with the divinity in your house.*

We must do whatever it takes to become a Bethany-kind of church, a Bethany-hearted people, and a family marked by the Bethany-kind of love and hospitality. Each one must learn how to chase God while serving man—how to worship Divinity while also serving humanity.

Where Is the Balance—Socially Active or Spiritually Passionate?

The Church is usually a little unbalanced because it is constantly torn between the practical and the spiritual. Most churches tend to lean toward one side or the other; they are either *socially active* or *spiritually passionate.* Very seldom do you find a church that manages to be *both,* and when you do, you have found a very unusual environment. If it is the kind of place where both God and man are comfortable, then it is also the kind of place where true revival is most likely to break out.

If God is comfortable there, then that church has genuine credibility in the heavens. If the church body is openly and actively compassionate about humanity, then it enjoys credibility on earth. God is searching for modern "houses of Bethany" that have credibility in *both* realms.

Real revival does not occur simply because God shows up. Obviously revival will never occur *unless* He comes, but have you asked yourself why revival didn't just spring up and why thousands of people didn't flock to the place where you encountered Him?

I remember attending and ministering in meetings with just 40 people where we had a real encounter with God. His presence was so tangible that we just wanted to stay there forever. The problem was that our encounter didn't seem to affect anyone besides the people who were there! I treasure those encounters with God's presence, but I'm convinced that God wants more—and I do too. I want nothing less than genuine revival to sweep across the world *outside* the church building.

Real revival does not occur simply because a lot of people show up for a meeting. Massive crowds of people show up for all kinds of things every day—they gather to see a circus and its side shows too. They flock to stock car races, dog races, cat shows, illegal dog fights, championship boxing matches, Little League baseball games, basketball games, high school football games, ice hockey matches, parades of all kinds, grand openings, Mardi Gras, and professional wrestling extravaganzas. None of these meet any reasonable definition of revival. They have lots of people but very little of God.

Revival has never been defined as a mass of humanity gathered in one place for one purpose. If that was the case, then humanity's mass gathering around the tower of Babel was really a revival meeting.[3] I don't think so.

REAL REVIVAL TAKES PLACE ON THE MIDDLE GROUND

Bethany represents the middle ground, the place where God and man meet together in an atmosphere of mutual comfort. Jesus always loved the middle ground, so it is no accident that real revival takes place there.[4]

Jesus died on the middle cross while suspended between Heaven and earth as a living intersection, the Door between human existence and eternity. When the manifest presence of the Reviver invades meetings filled with hungry people, He becomes the intersection between humanity and Divinity and produces what I call revival.

As we noted earlier, the cross of Christ depicts the divine balance we all seek, where compassion for humanity in the horizontal plane of our life intersects with passion for Divinity in the vertical plane of eternity. Yet the cross is planted deeply in the soil of everyday existence on planet Earth. For this reason, I believe *real revival is when both God and man show up at the same time and the same place.*

Unfortunately, most of us avoid going too deep in the vertical dimension or too far in the horizontal dimension. In fact, we usually don't "go" at all.

If outward appearances mean anything (and I doubt if they do), then most of the people in church on a weekend are making only nodding glances in God's direction. True holy hospitality will lead to deeper commitments and that dreaded four-letter word, w-o-r-k. True Marthas would be active in Sunday school work, children's church, the nursing home ministry, and Mother's Day programs, but most of us aren't.

REAL MARTHAS WORK; FAKE MARTHAS TALK

If we really were Marthas, we would be feeding and clothing the poor. You would find us pouring our time and energies into orchestrating all kinds of outreach programs in our cities and around the world. At the very least, you would run into us on Saturdays cleaning the church building, preparing communion trays for the next service, or baking peanut brittle to finance future missions trips. But since most of us are not real Marthas, you probably won't see much of us at all. Those who do show up would rather talk than work.

We have all of the form of Martha, while lacking the hard work and dedication found in the genuine article. We do just enough—usually through modest or minimal financial gifts dropped in the offering plate—to maintain the appearance of a Martha ministry. We talk the talk but don't walk the walk.

So if we aren't really Marthas, then that means we are really Marys, right? Perhaps. We still have a habit of glancing at our watches when certain people get more deeply involved in worship and prayer than we do. Many in our services face a real danger of developing "tennis elbow" from watch watching when the worship service spills beyond the acceptable noon hour.

The truth is that most of us maintain just enough of a façade in our planned worship services to give the appearance that we are really spiritual people. (Actually, some people admit the only thing they're really religious about is getting out the door on time.)

DESCRIBE YOUR PASSIONS, REVEAL YOUR SOUL

In general, we seem to be far more passionate about our hobbies, jobs, favorite sports, and leisure activities than we are about the Lord, the Church, or our spouse! I've noticed that many will talk at length about Mary's extravagant worship of Jesus' divinity or Martha's over-focused ministry to His humanity. Yet I have never heard anyone accuse either sister of harboring the error we stumble over the most—*arrogant apathy.*

I've carried a burden for this book for several years, but I didn't feel a release to write until the Holy Spirit specifically confirmed the time had come. At the same time I sensed a growing frustration in the Church. We all seem to be asking the question in different ways: *"How do you do find the balance between Mary's passionate worship to God and Martha's ministry to man?"*

I don't claim to have all the answers, but if perhaps I can frame the right questions, people will find their own way to the truth. Frankly, I pray this book sets off a firestorm of Bethanys where Mary and Martha sign a peace treaty and say, "We are going to work together in the same house so resurrection power will come to our city."

HOW DO YOU BUILD CREDIBILITY WITH GOD?

We make God "comfortable" by providing *furniture* and *food* suited for the habitation of Divinity. In *God's Favorite House*, I tell the story of a friend with an apparent genetic disorder that caused him to be extremely obese.

His great size and weight made it uncomfortable for him to visit the homes of his friends because none of them had furniture designed specifically to bear his weight. After some sad experiences with broken furniture and a broken heart, he learned to look through the door for furniture strong enough to hold him before agreeing to enter a home for a visit. My friend usually gave the prospective hosts some excuse, but he told me, "The truth is that I'm only leaving because there is no furniture in their house that can hold me."[5]

The Hebrew word translated as "glory" in the Old Testament is *kabod*. Its literal meaning is "weightiness or weighty splendor."[6] I ask the question in the book, "*I wonder how many times the 'weighty glory' of God has visited us but not come in?* How often does He stand at the back door of our assemblies with His glory still hidden by His 'hat and coat' while He scans the room, looking for a place to sit that will hold His weightiness?"[7]

The Old Testament type and shadow of "God's seat" is the mercy seat positioned between the cherubim on the ark of the covenant. The glory of God would descend to this area between the outstretched wings of the cherubim and remain there.

David elaborated on the spiritual reality behind the natural representation when he said God is "enthroned in the praises of Israel."[8] This puts us right back in the Mary position at Jesus' feet. This is how Mary created "furniture" so comfortable to Divinity that the Son of God preferred her throne of passionate tears to every throne of gold and precious gems on earth.

HOW DO YOU "FEED" GOD?

If our praises create a mercy seat for God's habitation, how do we "feed" Him? Once again, Jesus used Mary's sacrifice at a public meal to demonstrate how much He is attracted to the hunger and need of the human heart.

Like countless numbers of pastors, elders, and deacons in the Church today, the disciples got nervous when faced with such raw hunger for God and were saying, "Somebody stop this woman!" But Jesus intervened and said, "No, finally *somebody is doing something that's right.* Don't you dare stop her!" The Church doesn't make room for Marys with alabaster boxes because they make all the rest of us nervous when they begin to dismantle their glory, pride, and ego right there "in front of everybody."[9]

The Lord's encounter with the Samaritan woman at Jacob's well taught us that God seeks worshipers.[10] Yet there are other levels of worship and hunger revealed in Mary's ministry to Jesus that may transform our houses of worship into houses of divine habitation.

If He hears that cracking tinkle when you break your alabaster box of personal treasures; if He notices the rustling sound as you bow to dismantle your own glory; you are going to stop Him in the middle of whatever He is doing, because God cannot pass by a broken and contrite heart. He is going to move Heaven and earth just to come visit you.

If you want to know why some churches have revival, or why some people have intimacy when multitudes do not; the answer is that *these are people of brokenness.* The breaking of your heart arrests the ears and eyes of God, and it begins when your love for Him supercedes your fear of what others may think.[11]

WHY DO WE NEVER SEE REVIVAL?

If real revival comes when God and man both show up at the same time and the same place, then we should have enough sense to understand why so many churches and ministers never see revival.

I've been around some people who exhibit an unusual ability to perceive spiritual truth, declare divine purpose, and reveal a deep understanding of God's ways and nature. Yet the same people can hardly relate to "normal" people. It is very difficult to maintain a friendship with them because they won't contribute anything to the effort. They can make more people angry by accident than I can on purpose—and I'm pretty good at this!

Why is it so difficult to be around certain "super spiritual" people? The problem is that they don't have credibility in the human realm because they seem to care little whether other people live or die, prosper or perish. They see other people as bothersome distractions from their personal pursuits.

One of the people who taught me a great deal about the deeper things of the Spirit probably fit into this category. The first time I walked into a room to meet him, he turned to his grandson and said, "Is this who I have to talk to?"

I had just flown halfway across the country just to spend an afternoon with this great man of spiritual insight, but at that moment I felt more like a nuisance than a fellow minister in the faith. We met, nevertheless, and became good friends.

This man was very advanced in years, and I knew he wasn't always so distant from people. He had experienced incredible spiritual encounters in a life filled with risky and faith-stretching ministry that touched the world, and I was grateful for the opportunity to receive from him. At that point in his life, however, I had to pursue him rather than expect him to seek me out.

If You Know Him, You Should Make Him Known

The Church has always wrestled with the extreme attractions of intimacy with God to the exclusion of everything else. The ascetic school of thought held that the highest service to God was done in total isolation from all worldly distractions. For centuries monks have sequestered themselves from humanity in a quest for intimacy with Divinity. Although they produced many noteworthy scholarly works and insights, their ability to affect humanity was essentially non-existent. *If you know Him, you should make Him known.*

Salt as a food additive and preservative is supposed to affect whatever it touches. I seem to remember Jesus saying, "You are the salt of the earth; but if the salt loses its flavor, how shall it be seasoned? It is then good for nothing but to be thrown out and trampled underfoot by men."[12]

If God put something in you to pass on to others but you separate and segment yourself from society so that you never touch anybody, what good are you? You can worship God all day long, but what if He is trying to tell you, "I would really like to see some of the glory I poured into you released and sprinkled over someone else. You are My hands and feet in the earth, so carry My presence with you into the world of men"? Remember the words of Abba Silvanus, the fourth century monk we quoted earlier in the book, when he told his overly spiritual disciple: "Mary needs Martha. It is really thanks to Martha that Mary is praised." [13]

You will know you have credibility with man when you can call for humanity to come to your house for a visit, and the response is, "We can trust them. Why? Because they fed us when we were hungry and they clothed us when we were cold. They sheltered us when we were in need and they cared for us when we were sick. They even visited us in prison when no one else cared whether we lived or died."[14]

"THE CHURCH COULDN'T CARE LESS ABOUT US"

Some churches never affect their communities. They've given the people who live in them a distinct impression that says, in effect, "That church couldn't care less about us. All they care about is God, and He doesn't seem to care about us either or the folks who claim to be His people would show it." These churches have no credibility with their communities because they have no works to back their words.

They're asking the people in their communities to eat at their House of Bread without providing any incentive to investigate or any proof of their ability to bake the real thing.

Ask anyone who grew up near a bakery, "What do you remember most about the morning air in your neighborhood?" My guess is the answer will be, "I remember the smell of fresh baked bread and pastries. It was like stepping into a bakery shop every morning when I stepped outside. Yeah, there's nothing like fresh donuts in the morning…"

Imagine living beside a bakery that *did not* produce the fragrance of fresh-baked bread. Even worse, what if that bakery produced smells of rancid or burnt oil, the industrial smell of cleaning fluids, or the stench of rotting garbage?

PRETENDING ALONG LESSER-KNOWN HIGHWAYS

Churches that lack the basic fruit of God's love in action are like those odd eating establishments you see along lesser-known highways boasting expertise in styles of cuisine totally unrelated to their name, location, or apparent qualifications.

I would think twice before treating my family to a sumptuous meal at "Bubba's House of Authentic Fine French Cuisine" in Toadhead, Arkansas, or "McGruder's Taco and Knockwurst Shack" in Hampton, Virginia.[15] (In general, I also avoid virtually *any* "Genuine Cajun" entrée in restaurants located outside of Louisiana, unless of course an expatriate Louisiana Cajun is cooking in the kitchen. Even then, as a Louisiana native, I'd have to wonder why a real Cajun would leave the heavenly regions of home for anywhere else.) In food and in faith, *credibility* really matters.

Nearly two decades ago, my good friends, Bart and Coralee Pierce, went to Baltimore, Maryland, to start a church. Bart said the Lord told them, *"If you will take care of the ones nobody wants, I will send you the ones everybody is after."*[16] It makes sense, doesn't it?

Pastor Pierce started ministering to the drug addicts, to the gutter people, and to the down-and-outers whom nobody else wanted. Miracles soon followed and things began to improve in the city. Before long the up-and-outers started coming too.

When people see that you are compassionate to humanity, they quickly realize they can trust you because you have *earned* credibility in their realm by backing your words with works.

GREATER PASSION SHOULD PRODUCE GREATER COMPASSION

I've devoted most of my energies over the past few years to creating hunger for God's presence in the Church, but I am painfully aware that we will fail if our increased *passion* for God does not produce increased *compassion* for man.

For this reason, I am personally convinced that we have no right to decry abortion until we provide a practical solution. We can't tell teenage girls, "No, you shouldn't abort your babies," unless we're willing to say, "Yes, we'll take care of you by providing housing, prenatal care, and the full costs of the birth. Then we will help you find good candidates to provide a loving home for the baby."

If an inner-city church is tired of the prostitution ring on the corner, it must be prepared to support its biblical message of sexual purity and repentance from sin with an equally strong offer to take in, shelter, and disciple those who want to break free from the street trade.

Suburban churches weary of seeing their youth sucked into drugs must be prepared to do something positive about the problem. Police departments set up special units to investigate, infiltrate, and eliminate high-profile crime segments. Surely the Church can be just as aggressive and focused. We have the mind of Christ—surely we can find creative and effectives solutions to the sin problems in our community.

Until the Church comes to the place where divine passion and human compassion meet, there will be a credibility erosion. Nothing is accomplished when we merely point out the problem without providing solid solutions.

Pastor Pierce said, "I am convinced that reaching out to society's 'throw-aways,' the outcasts, and the destitute, the 'ones nobody wants,' is fundamental to the gospel. It is certainly a defining characteristic of genuine followers of Christ."[17]

Jesus Was Both Spiritual and Practical

Jesus established a precedent for valuing godly action at least as much as we value our gatherings and principles of godly living. Twice in the Gospel of Luke, Jesus answered rebukes from religious leaders for healing people on a religious day when they thought He should devote Himself to purely spiritual activities. He said:

> *"Hypocrite! Does not each one of you on the Sabbath loose his ox or donkey from the stall, and lead it away to water it? So ought not this woman, being a daughter of Abraham, whom Satan has bound—think of it—for eighteen years, be loosed from this bond on the Sabbath?"[18]*

In the sense that Mary and Martha are a *team*, it is true that helping the hurting is as much an act of worship as anything else. How can we expect people to accept our offer to supply food for their souls if they can't trust us to provide food for their bodies?

I'm not saying you have to feed everyone who comes along with a story and enough alcohol on their breath to pickle a cucumber while it's still on the vine. I learned this lesson the hard way as a young man helping my dad in De Ridder, Louisiana. My dad was the pastor, and I was helping out wherever I could.

My lesson came after the drunks around town discovered that I was a soft touch. Every time one of them knocked on the church door, I'd give him five dollars. (I was operating according to the Scripture that says, "Do not forget to entertain strangers, for by so doing some have unwittingly entertained angels.")[19] I didn't have a whole lot of money so I decided to extend the ministry using the church's petty cash fund.

Checking the Breath of Angels

One day my dad came to me and said, "Son, the word is that you're giving money to everybody who comes to the church door."

By that time I was handing out a lot of cash each week. I said, "Well, Dad, you never know—there may be an angel." He smiled and replied with his trademark humor, "You know, son, I seriously doubt if an angel reeks of alcohol." With a wink he added, "He might, but I don't think so." After that I evaluated all of my homeless visitors for angel status by the same criteria—I smelled their breath. It sounds like a silly mistake, but God blessed me in it anyway because I felt compassion for those men.

If you lose your ability to be compassionate toward man, your ability to be useful to God in the world is limited, no matter how passionate you become toward God. Why? It takes *both* Mary and Martha to entertain Divinity and humanity together *under one roof.* God wants to fellowship with humanity, and humanity desperately needs to fellowship with Divinity. *Our lives and our churches become the meeting ground at the point where passion and compassion meet in God's name.*

Humanity is blindly searching for its lost spiritual heritage and home. Jesus expressed the earthly problem of Divinity when He said, "Foxes have holes and birds of the air have nests, but the Son of Man has nowhere to lay His head."[20] Some churches have learned how to create a place where man can rest, and a few have even learned how to create a place where God can find rest. God is looking for a place where Divinity and humanity can rest together. Eden was lost long ago; it's up to us to *restore the garden of God in our churches—a place where God and man can walk and talk together.*

YOUR WEARY FLESH MAY BE SEATED

We may notice along the way that the intersection of passion for God and compassion for man can take some interesting turns *in our services.* While I was preaching at a large conference attended by thousands of people, the host pastor leaned over to say, "I feel like we're sort of stuck at a spiritual point in this service. I feel like we can't carry it to the next level."

The worship service was anointed, but the people had been standing for nearly two hours by that time, so I said, "Tell them to sit down."

"You mean you want to stop it?" he said.

"No, they're tired," I said. "Do you remember in the second chapter of the Book of Acts when the Holy Spirit fell so hot and heavy that it set their hair on fire? Look closely at the passage. *They were seated.*"

Then the pastor said, "Well, I don't want to dishonor what the Holy Spirit is doing."

I understood what the pastor was saying, but I said, "You won't dishonor God. I'll walk up to the podium and allow people to be seated." Then I talked to the people about maintaining their spiritual posture while they're seated, and we suddenly sensed the level of God's presence rise in the room. They were physically tired, but still wanted to pursue.

We cannot overlook the human factor in our corporate pursuit of God's presence. There are many Christian leaders who have the ability to lead people deeply into the realm of the Holy Spirit. The problem is that many of them fall into the disjointed parade syndrome. They get so far out in front of the God Chaser parade that they leave the people behind.

HUNGRY FOR GOD, HUNGRY FOR REST

Every minister and worship leader must remember that real people get tired sometimes (even Jesus had to take breaks). Most people work 8 hours on the job or 15 hours in the home before arriving at a Friday night meeting. Their spirits are hungry for God, but their bodies may be hungry for rest; so we must be aware of their hunger in both realms.

Jesus was always aware of the weariness of His followers. He took it upon Himself to cook the weary disciples a fish barbecue on the shore.[21] At least two times, Jesus was so aware of the humanity of the crowds following Him into wilderness areas that He interrupted His teaching to tend to their physical fatigue and hunger. Each time He had them *sit down* while He arranged a miracle to feed thousands using some fish and a few loaves of bread.[22] Jesus understood that it takes Mary's passion for Divinity and Martha's compassion for man to create the proper atmosphere where God and man can sit down together.

AVOID THE EVERLASTING TO ACQUIRE THE ETERNAL

You can never take people to places where they can't go physically. Just as it is unlikely that a 76-year-old grandfather with arthritis will ever climb to the summit of Mount Everest, it is nearly impossible to take people into God's presence when their stomachs are growling and the temperature is 130 degrees Fahrenheit. Things will change quickly if you erect a shelter to block the sun, give them a place to sit, and feed them. If Jesus did it, we can too. On a simpler level, my grandfather used to say, "A sermon doesn't have to be everlasting to be eternal."

I'm convinced God wants us to be normal and supernatural at the same time. In my opinion, the house of Mary and Martha presented a perfect blend of the two and together they made Jesus feel perfectly comfortable under their roof. The blend was simple: Mary entertained His divinity while Martha entertained His humanity.

It is hard to feed a man's soul when his belly is growling, and it is nearly impossible to tell a family about God's love when they are shivering in the cold without dry clothing or coats. The Church is surrounded by hurting humanity, and every need is an opportunity for miraculous ministry.

We serve a Master who plainly said He did not come to cure the whole, to feed the full, or heal the healthy.[23] If we make it our aim to accept and recruit only the whole, the full, and the healthy, then we may miss the one Visitor we need more than any other.

On the other hand, if we dare to chase God while serving the unlovely and unwanted, we are certain to see another Visitor enter our presence. He is unashamedly attracted to human need and spiritual hunger.

Endnotes

1. For more insights into the life-changing encounters that led David to build "God's favorite house," see the first chapter of my book, *God's Favorite House* (Shippensburg, PA: Fresh Bread, an imprint of Destiny Image Publishers, 1999), pp. 4-7.

2. 1 Timothy 2:4a.

3. See Genesis 11:1-9.

4. For more information about the importance God places on the middle ground, see "Part 1: Preserving the Middle Ground" in my book, *Answering God's Prayer: A Journal With Meditations From God's Dream Team* (Ventura, CA: Regal Books, a division of Gospel Light, 2000), pp. 13-24. This personal prayer and meditation journal was written specifically to accompany my book, *God's Dream Team: A Call to Unity* (Ventura, CA: Regal Books, a division of Gospel Light, 1999).

5. Tommy, *God's Favorite House*, p. 48.

6. James Strong, *Strong's Exhaustive Concordance of the Bible* (Peabody, MA: Hendrickson Publishers, n.d.), **glory** (#H3519, #H3513).

7. Tenney, *God's Favorite House*, p. 49.

8. Psalm 22:3b. I encourage you to read *God's Favorite House* for an in-depth study of the role of worship and praise in God's Kingdom and the way we enthrone God in our corporate gatherings.

9. Tommy Tenney, *The God Chasers* (Shippensburg, PA: Destiny Image Publishers, Inc., 1998), pp. 132-133.

10. See John 4:23.

11. Tenney, *The God Chasers*, p. 136.

12. Matthew 5:13.

13. This passage appears at the conclusion of a story quoted in Chapter 3. In addition to the citations noted in that chapter, it appeared in an article by Dennis Okholm, professor of theology at Wheaton College, printed in *Christianity Today*, September 4, 2000, p. 66. (Title of article unknown.)

14. See Matthew 25:31-46 for an even stronger indictment delivered by none other than Jesus Himself.

15. These alleged establishments are the products of my imagination, and the locations were chosen solely for their geographic positions far from regions recognized for the specific cooking styles mentioned. If any restaurants sporting these names actually exist, I extend my apologies and hope you are better able to back your claims than most of us in the Church can back ours.

16. Bart Pierce, *Seeking Our Brothers: Restoring Compassionate Christianity to the Church* (Shippensburg, PA: Fresh Bread, an imprint of Destiny Image Publishers, 2000), p. 3.

17. Pierce, *Seeking Our Brothers*, pp. 3-4.

18. Luke 13:15-16. See also Luke 14:5.

19. Hebrews 13:2.

20. Matthew 8:20.

21. See John 21:3-13.

22. See Matthew 14:19; 15:35.

23. See Matthew 9:12-13.

Chapter Eleven

Proximity Effect

The Side Benefits of Living Near a "Bethany"

Take a trip across any section of the United States, parts of Canada, and other places in the world, and watch for signs that claim certain towns are so special that you can't miss the opportunity to visit. The signs show up in the strangest places.

They may say, "See Lincoln's Birthplace," "The Proud Home of President So-and-So," or "Jesse James Buried Here." Others urge you to visit historical sites such as "the site of the Battle of Gettysburg," "the site of Custer's Last Stand," "The Home of the Alamo," "the site of the Battle of Waterloo" (in Belgium), or "the site of the Bridge Over the River Kwai" (at Kanchanaburi, Thailand).

The list seems endless but the purpose is always the same. Something happened or someone passed through these towns, cities, and geographical locations that transformed history. For some reason the event, person, and place would be linked together in future memory.

A friend of mine said that during his university years he used to eat at least twice a week at a little storefront diner with a wall-sized cartoon mounted behind the counter. The diner's claim to fame was that a famous syndicated cartoonist ordered at that counter many decades earlier while waiting for his child who attended the nearby university.

The cartoonist drew the owner a sketch of his trademark figure saying, "When I'm in Columbia, I eat at Joe's," or something to that effect. It wasn't long before the drawing was duplicated on the front wall and enshrined in local legend. That little diner enjoyed decades of notoriety and free advertising from a fleeting moment of fame lasting only the length of a meal.

Imagine for a moment how your life would change if Mary and Martha lived beside you and Jesus walked past your house every time He visited the sisters of Bethany. What were the side benefits received by the village of Bethany simply because the Son of God liked to visit two sisters and a brother who lived there?

Consider the Scripture passage that says, "And there are also many other things that Jesus did, which if they were written one by one, I suppose that even the world itself could not contain the books that would be written."[1]

How many miracles were performed (but not recorded) just in the vicinity of Bethany simply because our dual-natured Savior felt comfortable staying at Mary and Martha's house? Every time Divinity walked to Mary and Martha's house (and evidently it happened very often), His compassion for humanity went with Him. Do you believe He could pass by a sick child without reaching out to heal and comfort? How many times would the Man of compassion pass by the blind grandmother living next door before He stopped to restore her sight and demonstrate God's love?

HOW LARGE IS YOUR SHADOW FOR GOD?

I've been told that rabbinic tradition teaches that a man's anointing or influence only extends as far as his shadow will reach. That would imply the higher your position (or in our view, the closer you are to the Son), the greater your influence. The Bible is filled with references linking a person's shadow with his authority to provide shelter, protect, exert influence, and affect the lives of others.[2]

No one casts a longer "shadow" than Jesus. When He was nailed to the cross and hung high on the hill called Calvary, He cast a shadow that extended all the way from before the beginning of creation to beyond the end of time. That is a long shadow of influence.

Can you imagine waking up on mornings Jesus walked through Bethany to enter Mary and Martha's house of habitation? What kind of power surge swept through that place when the Son of God came to town? It makes me wonder if there were any sick people left in Bethany! Mary and Martha's house must have been one of the most popular and best-known places in the area. We know of at least one house that didn't survive His visitation in one piece.[3] (Desperate people think nothing of tearing off the roof of a house just to get to the Real Thing.)

What are the side benefits to any village, town, or city where someone creates an environment that is so comfortable to Divinity and humanity that the manifest presence of God is drawn there to meet and rest in the company of humanity? God did not send a robot to set us free; He sent His only begotten Son, and the Son of God was and is moved with *compassion* for people.[4]

What Is Going on Under Your Roof?

Think of the side benefits to *your* city and region if that environment is created in your home or church? How many miracles would come to your area if God finds Mary and Martha working together to chase God and serve man *under your roof*?

Bethany was blessed because Jesus had a place to rest where both His divinity and His humanity were served. What will happen if your church or home ever develops a resident environment where you are able to host the Holy Spirit? If you learn to make Him feel comfortable while also making humanity feel at home, then God's manifest presence may come to stay. What side benefits would that provide for *your* city and region?

We know that God doesn't necessarily "walk" to our meetings as Jesus did during His earthly ministry, but the proximity effect of the "divine shadow" still seems to apply. When the manifest presence of God enters a place and remains for any length of time, divine power seems to radiate and extend beyond the walls of a building and boundaries of a property to affect everything and everyone nearby.

Let me give you two examples of the proximity effect from the Bible. One deals with the power radiating directly from the Source of all power, and the other with the way divine power flows through ordinary people as we draw near to Him.

In *The God Chasers*, I described what happened when Jesus, the Son of God come in the flesh, stepped foot on the soil of a place totally given over to demon powers:

> When the sole of Jesus' foot touched the sandy shore of Gadara, one half-mile distant a man possessed of 5,000 demons suddenly was freed from their choking grasp for the first time. "Why? How do you know?" Mark tells us that when the demonized man saw Jesus, he ran to worship Him. Up until that precise moment, the demons had told him where to go and what to do at every other instance. He had no control over his own actions, even when the demons commanded him to cut himself.
>
> ...The true purpose of God's presence manifesting in our lives is *evangelism*. If we can carry a residue of God's glory back into our homes and businesses, if we can carry even a faint glow of His lingering presence into lukewarm churches, then we won't have to beg people to come to the Lord in repentance. They will run to the altar when His glory breaks their bondage (and they can't come any other way!).[5]

The second example demonstrates what happens when the God of More Than Enough manifests His presence through a typical man of "never enough." In this case, God used a rough, uneducated, and outspoken fisherman from a remote area to reveal His divine glory in Israel's greatest city. Revival broke out in Jerusalem the day the

Holy Spirit came to earth to stay, and the proximity effect took a strange turn in Peter's life at that point:

> ...*they brought the sick out into the streets and laid them on beds and couches, that at least **the shadow of Peter passing by might fall on some of them**. Also a multitude gathered from the surrounding cities to Jerusalem, bringing sick people and those who were tormented by unclean spirits, and they were all healed.*[6]

GOING PUBLIC WITH BURNING HEART AND SMOKING HAIR

The closer you walk to the Light of the World, the greater will be the shadow of spiritual influence you cast in the world. Peter walked out of the Upper Room and into the public eye with a burning heart and smoking hair after his encounter with the manifest presence of God. I wonder what would have happened if he had taken a stroll through the graveyards?

Have you ever sensed the presence of God rush into a meeting while you were worshiping Him? Think about all the people and places God had to "walk past" to descend on that meeting. I firmly believe that when God blesses one house in Bethany, Pensacola, Toronto, Houston, Baltimore, Kansas City, Pasadena, London, or Buenos Aires, then it is inevitable that many others are blessed by His procession as well.

"The closer you walk to the Light of the World, the greater will be the shadow of spiritual influence you cast in the world."

If you have an encounter with the presence of the Lord, don't be surprised when it *reaches out to affect the world around you.* New Age seekers would call it an aura; we know from the Scriptures and from the experiences of countless believers over the millennia that it is purely the presence of God resident in us—it has nothing to do with us and everything to do with Him.

Once you have a life-changing encounter with His presence, you become personally responsible for how you handle God's deposit in your life. The full weight of the parable of the talents comes to bear on your daily decisions and actions as a disciple of Christ.[7]

The cumulative obedience or disobedience of God's family often determines whether revivals and holy visitations extend into true habitations or are quickly cut short. When Martha joyfully serves humanity in God's name while encouraging Mary to minister to Divinity, God is drawn to the house. When the two appreciate one another and lay down their differences to make a permanent place for Him to dwell, divine visitation becomes divine habitation.

HAVE YOU LIMITED YOUR INFLUENCE?

We've already touched on this point, but it is crucial that we understand this danger: You may literally limit your influence in the earth if you fail to "cross over" when God says, "Mary, you must join Martha for a season," or "Martha, drop your serving towel and join Mary at My feet." The only way Bethany benefits from the Lord's presence is for Mary and Martha to work *together* to prepare a place of habitation.

Catch the vision of the potential of divine habitation in your home, church, or area. Imagine what could happen if you invest your deposit from God into someone else, and then the two of you work together to chase God while serving man. What if a whole roomful of people experiences an encounter with the living God and they begin to passionately minister to Him? How far will your supernatural compassion extend to the humanity nearby?

Envision a spreading canopy of God's glory extending beyond the confines of your apartment, church building, or auditorium to invade the bars, homes, apartment buildings, strip joints, businesses, and schools in a five-mile radius! This is revival the way God ordained it to be.

There is incredible power in corporate or "gathered" worship. It allows you to gather or pool the deposit from your God encounter with the deposits of other God Chasers who have "caught" Him. In

His grace, He helps us reach "critical mass" when our gathered cor-porate anointing from His presence brings a whole city under the influence of the Spirit!

When Mary and Martha work together to make a place of habi-tation for both God and man, the canopy of God's presence extends beyond every man-made or demon-inspired boundary. Nothing can stand in the way once the flood of God's glory begins to flow.

THE DIVINE PATTERN FOR PRESENCE EVANGELISM

God's manifest presence changes everything. I read somewhere that Jesus said, "And I, if I am lifted up from the earth, will draw all people to Myself."[8] Jesus was predicting the manner of His death, but I believe He also was sharing a divine pattern for what I call "presence evangelism." The incident with the demonized man is a perfect exam-ple of this, but there are countless modern-day examples as well.

During the revival that swept through the Hebrides Islands off the coasts of Scotland under the ministry of Duncan Campbell, God's presence exploded outward from a prayer meeting. Witnesses reported seeing men repenting behind haystacks in the fields and behind the doors of their houses where they had fallen to their knees in conviction—though not one word had been preached.

The local police officials asked Campbell to come to the station at 4:00 in the morning because so many people had gathered there to con-fess wrongdoing—it was the only thing they knew to do. As I wrote in *The God Chasers*, "The evangelist stood on the steps of the police station early that morning and preached the simple gospel of repentance and salvation through Jesus Christ and genuine revival came to that place."[9]

When God takes up residence in a person or place, everything becomes rearranged to center upon Him because He is the center of the energies in the universe. When Jesus humbled Himself to leave His place beside the Father to invade our world through the virgin birth in Bethlehem, all the universe was awaiting the cry of the new-born from Heaven. When He stepped into satan's playground in Gadara, the heavens and the earth delightedly watched Him destroy a lifetime of the enemy's work with a word.

WHAT HAVE YOU UNLEASHED IN YOUR COMMUNITY?

Can you imagine the heavenly influence unleashed in your community when you work with other God Chasers to build a house of habitation for the Holy Spirit? Who but God can say how many lives will be changed? How many people will be healed and delivered from an untimely and painful death tomorrow because a selfless group of God Chasers decide to say yes to God today? If earthly developers can create a new subdivision for man, why can't heavenly developers create a new place of habitation for God?

How many people will be touched by God because the Marys and Marthas in your church have agreed to work together in harmony to chase God while serving man? Remember that even the slightest concentration of God's presence in a human being or a group of people has noticeable consequences in the earthly realm:

- Moses stood in light of God's glory and his face glowed for days (Exodus 34:29-35).

- God touched Balaam's donkey and the speechless beast spoke to the spineless prophet, saving his life and sparing Israel from a curse (Numbers 22:27-33).

- Elijah the prophet called down the fire of Heaven and it consumed the water of earth (along with a blood sacrifice, water-soaked wood, and the stones of the altar) (1 Kings 18:1-39).

- The prophet Elisha, who carried a double measure of God's anointing, cut a stick and threw it into water to reverse the laws of physics and make an iron axe head float (2 Kings 6:1-7).

- Elisha's bones burned with so much of God's presence that, years after his death, they still held enough residue of Divinity that a dead man was raised back to life after his body was inadvertently dropped on top of the prophet's bones (2 Kings 13:21).

- At one word from Jesus, Peter the fisherman became Peter the water-walker, and we're still talking about it today (Matthew 14:28-29).

- After a ten-day prayer meeting, Peter the denier became Peter the soul winner, and God's power was so strong in him that people were even healed by his shadow (Acts 2:38-41; 5:15).

- A mere 30-second exposure to the glory of God's manifested presence motivated a former Pharisee and persecutor of Christians to preach the gospel despite being shipwrecked, whipped with 39 lashes on 5 occasions, and stoned and left for dead (Acts 9:1-22; 2 Corinthians 11: 23-27).

- Philip the table-waiter deacon was so filled with God's presence that he became Philip the Evangelist—and the first to travel to meetings by air (Acts 8:38-40).

What could happen and who could be touched if you pay the price to become a living habitation of God's manifest glory? What are the possibilities if your entire church accepts the dual mantle and call of Mary and Martha to build a habitation where Divinity and humanity can sit down together?

Endnotes

1. John 21:25.

2. See Song of Solomon 2:3; Lamentations 4:20; Isaiah 32:2; 51:16; Psalm 63:7.

3. See Mark 2:4, where the friends of a paralyzed man tore open the roof of a packed house to reach. Desperation gets results in the Kingdom.

4. See John 3:16; Hebrews 4:15.

5. Tommy Tenney, *The God Chasers* (Shippensburg, PA: Destiny Image Publishers, 1998), pp. 114, 116.

6. Acts 5:15-16.

7. See Matthew 25:13-30.

8. See John 12:32.

9. Tenney, *The God Chasers,* pp. 117-118.

Chapter Twelve

BUILDING A BETHANY

Where Passion and Compassion Intersect

Bethany appears to be the one place where Jesus the Son of Man and Jesus the Son of God felt comfortable. Why Bethany? Why not Nazareth where He grew up as a boy? Something made Jesus' divinity uncomfortable in Nazareth, because the Bible says He could do no mighty work there.[1]

In a sense, God would have been more comfortable in Nineveh than in Nazareth because, at the very least, the people of Nineveh repented and believed the words of Jonah the prophet. How can this be?

God's comfort level isn't based upon the geography or topology of a place. It has nothing to do with towering steeples, biblical themes rendered in artistic stained-glass splendor, plush carpet, or even the absence of these. Some people worship the primitive and say, "Oh, we've returned to the basics." Others who worship the luxurious may say, "Well, we want to make it look as pretty as we can for God."

God couldn't care less about any of these things. He is happy as long as Mary and Martha are in the house, whether the house is spacious and fitted with state-of-the-art furnishings or cramped and spare in design and décor.

Nineveh was an idolatrous town with a heathen environment, but God sent a prophet to extend mercy to Nineveh (though He still didn't make that city His home away from the heavenlies).

In contrast, Nazareth was the equivalent of America's Bible belt. Evidently racial prejudice was just as volatile in Nazareth as it has been in parts of our world today. The Lord's hometown folks went over the edge and tried to kill Jesus for implying that God had rejected Israelites who rejected Him while He worked miracles for non-Israelites who accepted Him.[2]

The pagan city repented and had a visitation of God (but no habitation). The hometown of the Son of Man rejected and dismissed the Reviver, bringing a curse upon itself.

Divine habitation has nothing to do with city limit signs or dollar signs; it has to do with human hospitality. The hospitality of Mary and Martha caused little Bethany to outshine Bethlehem, Nazareth, and Jerusalem (the places of His virgin birth, sinless maturity, and voluntary death on the cross). Evidently, the only other contender was a city called Capernaum, which means "village of comfort or consolation."[3]

Jesus stayed in Peter's home in Capernaum for a time after He was rejected by His hometown, Nazareth. It seems Peter's mother-in-law also knew how to host His divinity and humanity well.[4] Unfortunately, Capernaum (along with the towns of Chorazin and Bethsaida) followed in the footsteps of Nazareth and Jerusalem by rejecting Jesus while ignoring His many miracles (bringing a curse upon themselves in the process).[5]

THE TWO SISTERS OF HOSPITALITY OVERCAME THEIR DIFFERENCES

Only in Bethany did Jesus find someone who knew how to chase God while serving man. The two sisters of hospitality overcame their differences in focus, and it allowed them to jointly "carry the Dove" or to entertain Divinity in environments where no one else could. For example, their ability to serve man and anoint God was just as strong in Simon the leper's house across town as it was in their own home.[6]

The Church must become spiritually ambidextrous if it hopes to do the work of God by imitating the intercessory and priestly role of Jesus Christ in the heavenlies. With the left hand of Martha we extend godly compassion toward humanity and with the right hand of Mary we extend passionate love toward Divinity.

This requires us to be so credible and compassionate in the human realm that we can say, "Come meet Somebody," and the people in the community will listen and come. We must be so passionate in the spirit realm that we can say, "Lord, come meet somebody," and He will be pleased to take His seat in the throne of our praise while humanity gathers at His feet under the covering of our hospitality.

Our goal is to bring the two together in spiritual Bethany, where Mary and Martha serve God and man together. *If you can create an environment where Mary and Martha can get along, then you will have the credibility to call for Jesus and see Him raise your dead brothers.*

WHERE IS THE HOUSE WHERE GOD AND MAN MEET TOGETHER?

We see churches around the country where only God shows up to an isolated few, but quickly leaves their circle in search of more spiritual children. Even more churches have mastered the ability to serve humanity so well that only man shows up, for there is no provision for God on their agenda or in their hearts.

Where is the house where God and man show up at the same time at the same place? Where is the place in Bethany that captures the hearts of God and man in an unforgettable and continual banquet of adoration and faithful service? If the Marthas and Marys in the Church can ever live in peace, then divine visitation will become divine habitation and the world will never be the same.

God wants to move us from information to impartation, but it takes more than merely exchanging sermon notes as school children exchange notes in their classes. Impartation demands nothing less than trading heartbeats with the Father. We can only build Bethanys from the heart outward. Any other method produces imbalance or spiritual sterility. Paul's ministry exploded from the point of his encounter with God, not from his extensive theological data bank. Knowledge served Paul as a tool, but passion born in relationship motivated Paul as a human tool in the hand of God. God's Word equips us and guides us, but the same sterile religious system that trained Paul in the Scriptures also murdered the Messiah of the Scriptures. *Knowledge without relationship is deadly.* Know and study the Word of God, but above all be sure you know the God of the Word.

GOD WANTS BOTH MARY AND MARTHA IN THE HOUSE

Begin the construction of Bethany by seeking a divine encounter somewhere between Martha's kitchen and Mary's worship. Our goal is more than momentary or occasional visitation—it is nothing less than divine habitation.

The key is for God's people to cross the dividing line of passion and compassion and meet Him at the convergence of the cross—the single point in time and space where passion for His presence and compassion for His highest creation meet.

Although you and I may come from different backgrounds, we share one purpose: We want to recreate the comfort zone for God and man pictured in many places in the Scriptures—the Garden of Eden,[7] the tabernacle of David,[8] and Mary and Martha's house in Bethany.

"Lord, we pray with fervency: Come, Holy Spirit! But we also pray with fervency: Come, humanity."

Jesus chose to rest His head in the house in Bethany because of the balance Mary and Martha demonstrated as they cared for the needs of His humanity and His deity. This balance is foreshadowed in the most outstanding Old Testament type and shadow of God's manifested presence, the mercy seat on the ark of the covenant.

Technically, we shouldn't consider the mercy seat to be just one chair at all. The mercy seat was really a space, a place of residence situated between the outstretched wings of two cherubim on top of the ark.

HAVE YOU REMOVED THE MIDDLE GROUND?

God always comes to us in the *middle*, "where two or three are gathered together in My name."[9] If you look at the mercy seat on the ark of the covenant, the middle ground or place of habitation is lost the moment you take away one of the cherubim. It leaves Him no middle ground. If you take away one of the worshiping cherubim, you no longer have a mercy seat for the presence of God. All you have is a statue commemorating past visitations in a time of wholeness.

As I noted in the book, *Answering God's Prayer*,

> For some time I have been saying, "In revival, the size of the middle ground determines the size of the visitation." I later learned that A.W. Tozer saw this as well and wrote of it. This only reinforces my determination to pursue God's presence in the unity of the middle ground with other brothers and sisters, for I long for His habitation, not merely a momentary visitation.[10]

One human trait that severely limits revival is our tendency to control the things of God as if they were our own. This is another reason God manifests His presence in the middle ground. In *Answering God's Prayer,* I wrote, "God doesn't come to you, and He doesn't come to me. *He comes between us* so that *all of us* can touch Him but none of us control Him. He always searches for the middle ground."[11]

Jesus liked the controlled tension or interaction between Mary and Martha because He had the suspension bridge between them. Keep in mind that the house is not the most important component in Bethany's blessing. Mary and Martha could have lived in any house; it was the way the sisters worked together that made the house a home for Divinity and humanity. Mary and Martha recreated the same place of peace in Simon the leper's house in Bethany where Martha served and Mary anointed Him.[12]

KNOW WHEN TO DROP THE DUTIES AND DROP TO YOUR KNEES

Too many of us get derailed by the routines of house maintenance. You can repair the house in anticipation of visitation, but make sure you don't miss the moment of His coming! *Know when to drop the duties of the kitchen so you can drop to your knees before His face.* For some churches, the burden of taking care of the house of God crowded out the God of the house long ago.

How do you avoid that error? As we said earlier, let Martha be Martha and let Mary be Mary. The natural interaction between the two will create and preserve balance in the home that hospitality built.

Over the years, I've been amazed at the creativity displayed in the many Martha ministries of the Church. Some churches raise money for missions or for local benevolence ministries to the needy by making peanut brittle or baking pastries every Saturday. Some went so far as to make crepes—those thin pancakes people wrap around sweet fruit or rich meat and sauce fillings—and others sold crafts or held continuous yard sales. Some churches call their Martha ministry "the Ladies Auxiliary" while others call it simply "the ministry of helps." Regardless of the name, the heart of compassionate service to humanity was the same.

I don't know what traditions prevail in your local church, but it is probably safe to say that some of the same people who would willingly work all day long in a fund-raiser or church work day would be absent if you called a prayer meeting. There are exceptions, but they are the just that—exceptions.

In general, Marthas are virtually impervious to guilt trips about their aversion to extensive prayer efforts or overtly "spiritual" activities. Again, these Marthas love God as much as anyone else, but they are more comfortable in Martha's kitchen than in Mary's prayer closet. Don't try to make Martha fit into Mary's shoes or vice versa. Teach them how to live at peace with one another while validating one another's ministry.

DIVERSITY IS GOD'S GIFT

My marriage went to a new level the day I realized I was not going to train my wife to conform to my image. Thank God for that! It didn't take long for me to realize that she was different from me for a reason, and it would always be that way. At first I was bothered by the fact that we don't "see" the same things or feel the same way about everything. Then I realized that our diversity was God's gift to preserve and strengthen our marriage relationship.

In the same way, Martha and Mary aren't going to see the same need or feel the same way about things in your local church (or even in your home). Everyone has blind spots, and Marthas and Marys in the Church are equally oblivious to their individual blind spots and weaknesses. The truth is that they need each other for mutual protection and benefit.

They should be encouraged to talk to one another about their respective blind spots so they can avoid problems down the road. In the story I shared about driving on "the wrong side of the road" in the bus in England, the driver needed the help of others to cover his blind spots. Without their help, he might have crashed into other vehicles or objects while he negotiated the traffic in unfamiliar territory.

The coordination of Mary and Martha's ministry can take some interesting forms in the setting of a local church where all kinds of Mary meetings and Martha activities take place each week. A pastor may need to remind the Martha crew on Saturday, "I want to mention that last night the intercessory prayer group prayed for all of you. They really appreciate what each of you are doing here." This is just one way to validate the prayer ministry to "peanut brittle ladies" or "work day guys."

By the same token, the pastor may need to tell the Marys on Saturday night, "Let's go in there and lay hands on the peanut brittle stove," or "Let's encircle the outdoor pavilion the men are building and pray for the workers' safety and bless the work of their hands next week. They are really investing a labor of love in that place."

TEACH THEM HONOR OR CREATE A GROWING VOID

Either we teach Mary and Martha to honor one another's giftings, or we create a void filled with tension and disunity that will only grow worse with time. Jesus restored balance to the house when He said, "Now, Martha, calm down just a minute. Mary, it's okay. Mary has chosen the best part for right now."[13]

> *"Mary and Martha come together in His presence, and somewhere between Martha's kitchen and Mary's worship you are going to find Jesus.*

Now the honest truth is that you may never get everyone to participate in the Friday night prayer meeting, and you may never get everyone to roll out of bed and roll up their sleeves for the Saturday morning peanut brittle-making ministry. However, you should be able to get everybody together for a corporate worship gathering.

Mary and Martha come together in His presence, and *somewhere between Martha's kitchen and Mary's worship you are going to find Jesus.* The truth is, He probably has a broader definition of worship than we do. I suspect that He may even define peanut brittle making on Saturdays as a form of worship, because He honors the things you do "as unto the Lord."[14]

But don't let the burden of taking care of the house of God crowd out the God of the house. For some reason I'm convinced that the Martha who fixed the meal from the kitchen in Simon the leper's house was a different person from the Martha who complained about Mary from the kitchen in her own house early in Jesus' ministry. She was still Martha, but she had taken a trip to the other side. She had tasted the wonder of Mary's position and appreciated it as never before.

MARTHA MINGLED HER TEARS WITH MARY'S

As she prepared this *last* meal for Jesus, Lazarus, and Simon's other guests, I'm certain that Martha mingled her own tears of sweet sacrifice and adoration with Mary's. Martha's tears of worship and adoration, however, fell into the bread she made for His humanity. Her salty tears washed the fruit of the vine and anointed the meat she would offer Him.

This time, Martha's selfless service and approving support became the golden ring perfectly showcasing the diamond of Mary's gift of anointing for the Master's burial.

What she could she did. She honored Jesus, not by words but by deed; her act declared that his name was to her like ointment poured forth, and more precious [by] far than India's costliest spikenard. The precious alabaster, crushed by grateful hands, filled with sweetest perfume all the house in Bethany; and the record of it fills all the house of God on earth with heavenly odor. Her deed can add no fragrance to the death of Jesus, but it has borrowed everlasting fragrance from that death. Her act of anointing has been so linked with the burial of the Lord's Anointed, that it retains throughout the church the sweet savour of Christ's sacrifice having lent its perfume for ever to the good work of Mary.[15]

MARY OF THE KITCHEN JOINS MARTHA OF THE BENT KNEE

Martha was now the "Mary of the Kitchen," and Mary had become the "Martha of the bent knee" before Him. Together, *the sisters from Bethany* joined with *their brother from the grave* to give Jesus a send-off no one else could begin to equal. The meal may have taken place in Simon's house, but the chief source of natural comfort, human love, and spiritual nurture once again came from the household of Mary, Martha, and Lazarus.

Is it possible that this is yet another application of the ancient passage, "Though one may be overpowered by another, two can withstand him. And a threefold cord is not quickly broken"?[16] *No one but the Master knows just how much He needed the ministry of Mary, Martha, and Lazarus on the night before He began the lonely walk to the cross in Jerusalem.*

As you build your Bethany, remember the first lesson learned in the original house in Bethany. What takes first position in the priority list when God's manifested presence enters the house? Drop everything when the Master's presence comes through the door and minister to your First Love.

A.W. Tozer said, "Adoration is the lost art of worship in the church," and God wants to see this aspect of worship restored to the Church. What is adoration? Babies are our best tutors on the subject of adoration, but young children do a pretty good job too. Although my youngest daughter at times tells me, "Dad, you tell too many stories about me," I will share another incident that God used to teach me about adoration.

During her preschool years, my youngest daughter expected me to rock her to sleep every night when I was home. I spent 45 minutes with my wiggling, giggling girl each night, and sometimes she wanted to eat cereal in my lap. That could get really messy, but I was glad to put up with it all for just 30 seconds in Daddy paradise. That is how I describe those precious moments just before she fell asleep.

BATHED IN PURE ADORATION

She used to lie back against my chest and turn her face just right so she could look straight into my eyes. Then she would get a little smile on her face as the frantic pace of her thoughts slowed down and sleep overtook her. In a matter of moments, she was too sleepy to talk but her eyes just poured liquid love into my heart. I was being bathed in pure adoration in those moments.

Although my daughter is older now, it again happened while I was ministering on this subject at a conference and working on the book. I agreed to take my daughter to the hotel pool, and I also told my editor and some other people they could join me in the pool area that afternoon. I swam a little and climbed out of the pool to talk briefly with my visitors about the book. Then my little girl said, "Dad, quit talking to those people and come play with me." I admit I was kind of torn back and forth, but finally they all left and it was just my daughter and I in the pool.

We played just like two little kids. I would swim under water and she'd ride on my back, and every other game we could think of. Finally, I came up for air and she just fell over in my arms and looked at me with that unforgettable gaze of liquid love again. She didn't have to say anything; she just poured out her adoration. Then she said what every father loves to hear, "You are a great daddy."

DID YOU LOSE ADORATION IN THE LAUNDRY LIST?

Adoration demands participation from both Mary *and* Martha. It tends to get lost in the religious laundry list of most church services. We are so busy presenting things, announcing things, collecting things, and teaching things, that we forget to say to the Author and Finisher of our faith, "We love You. You are a great daddy. There is no one like You." God puts up with a lot just to get 30 seconds of pure adoration from His children.

Why don't we dispense with the formalities and just gaze into His eyes? "How do you do that?" All I know is that the posture of your heart is more important than the posture of your body. Do what it takes to assume the Mary position of adoration. You may need to close your eyes to look into His eyes. You may be more comfortable kneeling, standing, or lying prostrate before Him. Do what you have to do to tell Him from your heart, "I love You."

Martha, you've prepared in advance for this moment; now drop the dishtowel and put aside the food preparation duties. The Bread of Life is waiting for you to come to *His* table. Mary, you are already in the position of adoration. Now take a moment to encourage Martha to join you at His feet—but do it with humility, love, and full appreciation of Martha's gifts. Her labor of love set the table and created the opportunity for your gift to Him.

If the two of you continue to pursue His divinity while serving humanity, there is no reason for the feast to end. As long as your hearts stay passionately hungry for His presence, and as long as you reach out to meet humanity's needs in the house, His presence will not lift. He will take you from glory to glory as you behold His face.[17] Visitation can turn into habitation.

TAKE HIS PRESENCE WITH YOU

Although you must part temporarily in the natural so you can raise your families and maintain your jobs, make sure you take His presence with you as you go about your business. People who have consistently resisted your arguments or Christian witness will suddenly be undone by the divine deposit in your spirit. They will say about you what they said about Peter and John, "They have been with Jesus."[18] Don't be surprised when they say, "What has happened to you? How do I go get what you've got?"

It is like becoming a duet for Divinity in which Martha serves and Mary anoints. It's like singing in harmony: you sing the same song, but different parts. It is the epitome of chasing God and serving man. *The day Mary and Martha learn how to work together in your house is the day Bethany is built in your city.* The day God's presence enters your house is the day your city begins to change. Don't stop or let up now: Keep chasing God while serving man. Now seal the work of the Holy Spirit in your heart with this prayer:

> *Father, I feel a constant tug of war inside of me. Sometimes I don't know whether to worship or to do good works. I am concerned about what I see around me, and I'm concerned about what I feel above me in the spirit, but I don't have the wisdom to know the difference between the two.*
>
> *There is a kaleidoscope of backgrounds, gifts, abilities, and needs in the local church, Lord, and we need Your help if we ever hope to work together to build You a habitation.*
>
> *Father, make us passionate and set our hearts on fire with hunger for You. I also ask that You raise our compassion level. It is no wonder that the Church doesn't venture into the realm of the miraculous, Lord—we've neglected our brothers, and You can't bless our neglect.*
>
> *Lord, help us build a Bethany, a house of balanced passion and compassion. Teach us Your ways, Lord. Help me, and help everyone in the local church, to live with the tension between the Mary and Martha inside of us. Guide us to the resident place of the dove somewhere between Mary's posture of worship and Martha's kitchen.*
>
> *We must touch both if we are to become a bridge between two worlds. Help us, Lord. Don't let us become calloused. Father, forgive me for every time I've been insensitive to You and to man. I purpose to guard my heart and stay tender.*
>
> *We are building a Bethany house for You, Lord. We will chase You in passionate pursuit, yet we also will reach out to humanity in compassionate service. Come, Holy Spirit, and draw all men to Jesus as we lift Him up in our house of hospitality. Amen.*

Epilogue

I t is very important to take action when you are touched by truth. *God is waiting to be worshiped and man is waiting to be served.*

Chase God—passionately pursue Him. He desires your worship.

Serve man—compassionately serve him. Volunteer for your local food bank, help at a shelter. Find a need and meet it.

The earth needs more Marthas; the heavens need more Marys.

This is the official altar call of this book. It is time for Martha's hands to get dirty and Mary's knees to get calloused.

Endnotes

1. See Matthew 13:54-57; Luke 4:16-30.

2. See Luke 4:24-30.

3. James Strong, *Strong's Exhaustive Concordance of the Bible* (Peabody, MA: Hendrickson Publishers, n.d.), **Capernaum**, Hebrew definitions #2584, 3723, and 5151.

4. See Luke 4:31-39.

5. See Matthew 11:21-24.

6. See Luke 10:38-42 (at Mary and Martha's house); and Matthew 26:6-13; Mark 14:3-9; John 12:1-8 (at Simon's house).

7. See Genesis 3:8. That Adam and Eve used to join God during His garden walks seems to be implied but remains unstated. The Lord apparently wasn't surprised that they heard His voice or were in the garden; He was concerned about their fear (unknown until sin entered their hearts), their act of hiding, and their disobedience.

8. See 2 Samuel 7:18-21,25-29, where David *sits before the Lord* (before the ark of the covenant) after Nathan the prophet told him he wouldn't build a permanent or fixed house for God. Also see Acts 15:16-17, where God says He will rebuild the tabernacle of David, which has fallen. God and man met together freely in David's tabernacle, but this never happened on a public scale in the permanent buildings made for God.

9. Matthew 18:20a.

10. Tommy Tenney, *Answering God's Prayer* (Ventura, CA: Regal Books, a division of Gospel Light, 2000), p. 23. This chapter will be added to *God's Dream Team*, casebound edition, Spring 2002.

11. Tenney, *Answering God's Prayer*, p. 16. This chapter will be added to *God's Dream Team*, casebound edition, Spring 2002.

12. See Matthew 26:6-13; Mark 14:3-9; John 12:1-8.

13. This is my modern paraphrase of Luke 10:41-42.

14. This principle is revealed in Ephesians 6:5-9.

15. A. Moody Stuart, *The Three Marys* (Carlisle, PA: The Banner of Truth Trust, 1984), p. 197.

16. Ecclesiastes 4:12.

17. See 2 Corinthians 3:18.

18. See Acts 4:13.

GodChasers.network is the ministry of Tommy and Jeannie Tenney. Their heart's desire and ministry mandate is unifying the Body of Christ and pursuing the presence of God—not just in churches, but in cities and communities all over the world.

How to contact us:

By Mail:

GodChasers.network
P.O. Box 3355
Pineville, Louisiana 71361
USA

By Phone:

Voice: 318.44CHASE (318.442.4273)
Fax: 318.442.6884
Orders: 888.433.3355

By Internet:

E-mail: GodChaser@GodChasers.net
Website: www.GodChasers.net

Join Today

When you join the **GodChasers.network** we'll send you a free teaching tape and our ministry letter!

If you share in our vision for personal and corporate revival and want to stay current on how the Lord is using GodChasers.network, please add your name to our mailing list. We'd like to keep you updated on the fires of revival being set around the world through Tommy and the GodChasers team! We ll also send schedule updates and make you aware of new resources as they become available.

Run with us by calling or writing to:

Tommy Tenney
GodChasers.network
P.O. Box 3355
Pineville, Louisiana 71361-3355
USA

318-44CHASE (318.442.4273)
or sign up online at www.GodChasers.net/lists/

We regret that we are only able to send regular postal mailings to U.S. residents at this time. If you live outside the U.S. you can still add your postal address to our mailing list you will automatically begin to receive our mailings as soon as they are available in your area.

E-mail Announcement List

If you d like to receive information from us via e-mail, just provide an e-mail address when you contact us and let us know that you want to be included on the e-mail announcement list!

Chase God With Us
Daily E-mail Bible Reading Program
An Invitation to Run

If you already have a daily Bible reading plan, we commend you. If you don t we invite you to join with us in reading God's Word. Just go to our website @www.godchasers.net and click on Chase God to sign up and you will start receiving the daily reading! It only takes a few minutes each day to read the Bible in a year. Just find today s date and continue faithfully for the next twelve months.

If you skip a day, don't get discouraged. Don't let minor setbacks become major obstacles. Remember that the goal isn't to follow a "schedule" religiously; the goal is to spend time with God in His Word.

If you find yourself missing days fequently and are tempted to give up altogether, Don't! Disregard the dates and simply read a portion whenever you can. You may not feel like you're making progress, but as you move forward through more and more of the readings, you'll see how far you re really getting and be encouraged to continue.

God Chasers Ministry Internship

I m excited to announce a brand new GodChasers Internship Program for teenagers and young adults. I want to train the next generation of GodChasers so they can pass on this passion to their friends and communities! This year-long program will include classroom time, practical application and an opportunity to accompany my traveling team on a ministry trip. This isn t a summer camp or vacation—it will be hard work. It will involve a lot of sacrifice. Participants will be challenged and stretched and taken far beyond their comfort zones. It will be an intense, no-nonsense, power-packed time. Real work! Real ministry! Real destiny!

Tony

AUDIOTAPE ALBUMS BY

Tommy Tenney

FANNING THE FLAMES
(audiotape album) $20 plus $4.50 S&H

Tape 1 — The Application of the Blood and the Ark of the Covenant: Most of the churches in America today dwell in an outer-court experience. Jesus made atonement with His own blood, once for all, and the veil in the temple was rent from top to bottom.

Tape 2 — A Tale of Two Cities—Nazareth & Nineveh: What city is more likely to experience revival: Nazareth or Nineveh? You might be surprised....

Tape 3 — The "I" Factor: Examine the difference between *ikabod* and *kabod* ("glory"). The arm of flesh cannot achieve what needs to be done. God doesn't need us; we need Him.

KEYS TO LIVING THE REVIVED LIFE
(audiotape album) $20 plus $4.50 S&H

Tape 1 - Fear Not: To have no fear is to have faith, and that perfect love casts out fear, so we establish the trust of a child in our loving Father.

Tape 2 - Hanging in There: Have you ever been tempted to give up, quit, and throw in the towel? This message is a word of encouragement for you.

Tape 3 - Fire of God: Fire purges the sewer of our souls and destroys the hidden things that would cause disease. Learn the way out of a repetitive cycle of seasonal times of failure.

NEW!
WHAT'S THE FIGHT ABOUT?
(audiotape album) $20 plus $4.50 S&H

Tape 1 - Preserving the Family: God's special gift to the world is the family. If we don't preserve the family, the Church is one generation from extinction. God s desire is to heal the wounds of the family from the inside out.

Tape 2 - Unity in the Body: An examination of the levels of Unity that must be respected and achieved before "Father, let them be one" becomes an answered prayer!

Tape 3 - What's the Fight About?: If you re throwing dirt, you're just loosing ground! In **What's the Fight About?** Tommy invades our backyards to help us discover our differences aren't so different after all!

TURNING ON THE LIGHT OF THE GLORY
(video) $20 plus $4.50 S&H

Tommy deals with turning on the light of the glory and presence of God, and he walks us through the necessary process and ingredients to potentially unleash what HIs Body has always dreamed of.

THREE NEW VIDEOS BY

LET'S BUILD A BONFIRE VOL. 1:
LET IT FALL
(video) $20 plus $4.50 S&H

One hour of the best worship and word
from the GodChaser gatherings.

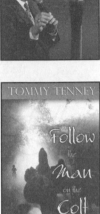

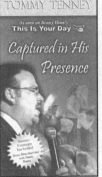

CAPTURED IN HIS PRESENCE
(1 hour video)
$25 plus $4.50 S&H

An encounter with God captured on tape as
seen on *This Is Your Day* with Benny Hinn.

FOLLOW THE MAN ON THE COLT
(1 hour video) $20 plus $4.50 S&H

Are you too proud to ride with Him? Humility
is the catalyst that will move your answers
from a crawl to a walk to a run and to a ride.

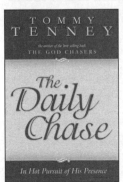

Tommy Tenney has touched the heart of a genera-tion who crave for an encounter with their Lord. The passion of his heart, captured in his writings, has ignited a flame of godly pursuit across this world.

The Daily Chase offers you the best of those writ-ings. Each day there awaits you a fresh encounter with the One you long for. Don't hold anything back.

Sample God Chaser Worship CD˙ enclosed in back of book includes:

• Sample songs from Jeannie Tenney's album "Holy Hunger"

• Sample songs from a NEW God Chaser worship album

• Sample video clips from the accompanying music video

*1st printing only

Elegant Case Bound Edition, $19.00

Run With Us!

Become a GodChasers Monthly Revival Partner

Two men, a farmer and his friend, were looking out over the farmer's fields one afternoon. It was a beautiful sight—it was nearly harvest time, and the wheat was swaying gently in the wind. Inspired by this idyllic scene, the friend said, "Look at God's provision!" The farmer replied, "You should have seen it when God had it by Himself!"

This humorous story illustrates a serious truth. Every good and perfect gift comes from Him: but we are supposed to be more than just passive recipients of His grace and blessings. We must never forget that only God can cause a plant to grow—*but it is equally important to remember that we are called to do our part in the sowing, watering, and harvesting.*

When you sow seed into this ministry, you help us reach people and places you could never imagine. The faithful support of individuals like you allows us to send resources, free of charge, to many who would otherwise be unable to obtain them. Your gifts help us carry the Gospel all over the world—including countries that have been closed to evangelism. Would you prayerfully consider becoming a revival partner with us? As a small token of our gratitude, our Revival Partners who send a monthly gift of $20 or more receive a teaching tape and ministry letter every month. This ministry could not survive without the faithful support of partners like you!

Stand with me now—so we can run together later!

In Hot Pursuit,

Tommy Tenney

Tommy Tenney
& The GodChasers.network Staff

Become a Monthly Revival Partner by calling or writing to:

Tommy Tenney/GodChasers.network
P.O. Box 3355
Pineville, Louisiana 71361-3355
318.44CHASE (318.442.4273)

More titles
by Tommy Tenney

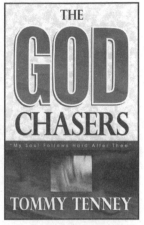

THE GOD CHASERS (National Best-Seller)
There are those so hungry, so desperate for His presence, that they become consumed with finding Him. Their longing for Him moves them to do what they would otherwise never do: Chase God. But what does it really mean to chase God? Can He be "caught"? Is there an end to the thirsting of man s soul for Him? Meet Tommy Tenney—God chaser. Join him in his search for God. Follow him as he ignores the maze of religious tradition and finds himself, not chasing God, but to his utter amazement, caught by the One he had chased.
ISBN 0-7684-2016-4
Also available in Spanish
ISBN 0-7899-0642-2

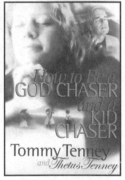

HOW TO BE A GOD CHASER AND A KID CHASER
by Tommy Tenney and Thetus Tenney.
One of the great challenges for the modern parent is how to make room for your personal pursuit of God in the midst of the pressing priorities of raising a family. *How to Be a God Chaser and a Kid Chaser* offers many practical answers to this challenging issue. Those answers come from a diverse background of writers including Thetus Tenney, Tommy Tenney, Ceci Sheets, Cindy Jacobs, Beth Alves, Jane Hansen, Dick Eastman, Wesley and Stacey Campbell.
ISBN 0-7684-5006-3

GOD'S FAVORITE HOUSE
The burning desire of your heart can be fulfilled. God is looking for people just like you. He is a Lover in search of a people who will love Him in return. He is far more interested in you than He is interested in a building. He would hush all of Heaven's hosts to listen to your voice raised in heartfelt love songs to Him. This book will show you how to build a house of worship within, fulfilling your heart's desire and His!
ISBN 0-7684-2043-1

Available at your local Christian bookstore.

For more Information and sample chapters, visit www.destinyimage.com

Foundationally Spirit-filled. Biblically Sound. Spiritually Inspirational.

━ THE IMPASSIONED SOUL

by Morton Bustard.

What mysterious force lifts a person out of the mainstream of mediocrity into the lonely pursuit of the heavenly vision? It is passion. Passion is the energy of the soul and the fire of life. Passion leads you to a life that will end the drought in your inner being. *The Impassioned Soul* comes to you as a cup of cool water for the thirsty pursuer. As its refreshing words touch your scorched soul, you will feel the energy of its life revitalizing all the parched places.

ISBN 0-7684-2113-6

━ GOD: A GOOD FATHER

by Michael Phillips.

In this startling book, Michael Phillips challenges the established Christian to step out of the status quo and into a breathtaking new relationship with God the Father. In a style reminiscent of John Bunyan s classic *Pilgrim's Progress*, Phillips acts as a "guide" on a journey to the place of the presence of our heavenly Father. A "divine restlessness" will stir your heart as you follow Michael Phillips out of the "fogbound lowlands" of our typical existence and you climb to the "mountain home of *Abba* Father," learning to know Him— His love, His goodness, His trustworthiness, His forgiveness—and choosing to live in His heart and drink of His water of life forever!

ISBN 0-7684-2123-3

━ POWER OF A COVENANT HEART

by David Huskins.

In a day when relationships are discarded for the smallest of excuses, Christians can demonstrate the gospel through covenant relationships to which they are joyfully committed. As we move into the new millennium, the enemy's greatest fear is that the Church will grow up and build unbreakable covenant relationships against which he has no power. In this extraordinary book, Bishop Huskins takes a fresh look at the covenant model of David and Jonathan. Each stage of David's life reveals another piece of the covenant heart. From this model, Bishop Huskins unveils the beauty and power of a covenant heart.

ISBN 0-7684-2116-0

━ THE PURPOSE AND POWER OF GOD'S GLORY

by Dr. Myles Munroe.

Everywhere we turn, we are surrounded by glory. There is glory in every tree and flower. There is the splendor in the rising and setting sun. Every living creature reflects its own glory. Man in his own way through his actions and character expresses an essence of glory. But the glory that we see in Creation is but the barest reflection of the greater glory of the Creator. Dr. Munroe surgically removes the religious rhetoric out of this most-oft used word, replacing it with words that will draw you into the powerful presence of the Lord. *The Purpose and Power of God's Glory* not only introduces you to the power of the glory but practically demonstrates how God longs to see His glory reflected through man.

ISBN 0-7684-2119-5

Available at your local Christian bookstore.

For more information and sample chapters, visit www.destinyimage.com

8 TT

Additional copies of this book and other
book titles from DESTINY IMAGE are
available at your local bookstore.

For a complete list of our titles,
visit us at www.destinyimage.com
Send a request for a catalog to:

Destiny Image® Publishers, Inc.
P.O. Box 310
Shippensburg, PA 17257-0310

*"Speaking to the Purposes of God for This
Generation and for the Generations to Come"*